PRAISE FOR CATHERINE HICKEM AND
HEAVEN IN HER ARMS

"The angelic message to Mary totally turned her world upside down. She was a gentle, reflective young woman who, dare I say, was also gutsy in her bravery. Reading Catherine Hickem's book encouraged, challenged, and inspired me about how to live my faith more exuberantly. Catherine's unique insights provide compelling reasons to see Mary as a valuable role model for all circumstances whether they're upside down or right side up. I am honored to commend this book to you; quite simply, it is brilliant."

> —Marilyn Meberg, Women of
> Faith speaker and author of
> numerous books, including her
> newest title *Constantly Craving*

"Catherine is a lovely combination of wisdom and grace. She's the kind of spiritual mentor you not only learn from, but also want to hang out with at Starbucks!"

> —Lisa Harper, author and
> Women of Faith speaker

Heaven in Her Arms

Heaven in Her Arms

*Why God Chose Mary to Raise His Son
and What It Means for You*

CATHERINE HICKEM

THOMAS NELSON
Since 1798

NASHVILLE DALLAS MEXICO CITY RIO DE JANEIRO

Published in Nashville, Tennessee, by Thomas Nelson. Thomas Nelson is a registered trademark of Thomas Nelson, Inc.

Thomas Nelson, Inc., titles may be purchased in bulk for educational, business, fund-raising, or sales promotional use. For information, please e-mail SpecialMarkets@ThomasNelson.com.

Unless otherwise indicated, Scripture quotations are taken from THE NEW KING JAMES VERSION. © 1982 by Thomas Nelson, Inc. Used by permission. All rights reserved.

Scripture quotations marked NASB are taken from the NEW AMERICAN STANDARD BIBLE®, © The Lockman Foundation 1960, 1962, 1963, 1968, 1971, 1972, 1973, 1975, 1977, 1995. Used by permission.

Scripture quotations marked ESV are taken from THE ENGLISH STANDARD VERSION. © 2001 by Crossway Bibles, a division of Good News Publishers.

Scripture quotations marked NIV are taken from the Holy Bible, New International Version®, NIV®. © 1973, 1978, 1984 by Biblica, Inc.™ Used by permission of Zondervan. All rights reserved worldwide. www.zondervan.com

Scripture quotations marked NLT are taken from the Holy Bible, New Living Translation, © 1996. Used by permission of Tyndale House Publishers, Inc., Wheaton, Illinois 60189. All rights reserved.

Names and identifying details have been changed, when appropriate, to protect the identities of those discussed in this book.

Library of Congress Cataloging-in-Publication Data

Hickem, Catherine, 1958-
  Heaven in her arms : why God chose Mary to raise his son and what it means for you / by Catherine Hickem.
    p. cm.
  Includes bibliographical references and index.
  ISBN 978-1-4002-0036-8 (alk. paper)
  1. Mary, Blessed Virgin, Saint. I. Title.
  BT603.H53 2011
  232.91—dc23   2011026710

Printed in the United States of America

12 13 14 15 16 QG 6 5 4 3 2 1

To my parents, Harold and Mary Ann Taylor, the first people who taught me how much Jesus loves me and who have lived lives reflective of Him every day of my life

CONTENTS

Contents

PROLOGUE

As a little girl, I would get excited when the Christmas season arrived. Like most children anticipating the big day, I loved all the activities leading up to Christmas. Decorating the tree, baking cookies, and singing Christmas carols were just a few of the rituals I looked forward to with my family.

While the activities were filled with fun and enlivened the holiday, celebrating the true meaning of Christmas took precedence. My father was the pastor of our church and understood the significance of using the Christmas season to love on people who might be alone, invisible, or hurting. As a result, the church calendar was packed with opportunities to celebrate the birth of Jesus and take the good news of His nativity to those in our community who were less fortunate.

Most years, prior to Christmas, our church had a pageant. I would sit in the pew next to my mom, transfixed as each character entered the church, as if the story were unfolding for the first time. Stillness filled the air, a reverence for the most significant event in history. I can still remember my little heart beating quickly, fascinated that kings would bow to a baby.

While I adored the nativity story, I was most fascinated with Mary, the mother of Jesus. I secretly wished I could play her role, even though I was a child myself. I was drawn to this woman, the only female mentioned in the birth scriptures, who year after year reminded us of the humanity of Jesus' birth and life. I felt pulled toward the vulnerable state of her pregnancy, her youthfulness, and the mystery of her selection as mother to the Son of God.

This strong alliance with Mary served to solidify my deep longing to be a mother myself. I was an only child for six years, and as a result, I had to learn how to play by myself. Nine times out of ten, I would play with my dolls, each of whom had a name, a story, and a personality. More than anything in the world, I wanted to be a mother when I got older. That deep urge never left me for a moment and would become a driving force in my life.

As I grew, I noticed that Mary was rarely mentioned. Occasionally, her name would come up when someone taught on the wedding in Cana, or the cross, when Jesus gave her care and protection over to His disciple John. But she was never the center of a story, just an appendage to the central truth being taught, unless it was at Christmas. Even then, she was never fully acknowledged for who she was and what God saw in her.

As the years went by and I became familiar with the differences in the ways people celebrate their faith, I noticed a tension between Protestants and Catholics regarding Mary's role. The Catholic faith enthusiastically embraces Mary and places great priority on her role. She is viewed as the mother of not only the Son of God, but of God. Her place in the Catholic Church is sacred, second only to that of Christ Himself.

On the other hand, in an effort to maintain the focus on Jesus and His divinity, few in the modern-day evangelical church have closely examined who Mary was and why she was chosen to be the mother of Christ. Scripture is filled with multiple role models of godly men who dared to live boldly for their faith, but there are far fewer women mentioned who did likewise. A study of Mary's life reveals key lessons about faith, dependency, and obedience to God. God's personal selection of Mary to be the mother of His Son is worthy of our faithful attention.

By allowing Mary to show up on the radar screen of faith only during the Christmas season, we are removing a role model for women and mothers of all ages and stages of life. To simply view her as a woman who bore the Son of God but had little to do with His development as a person and a man, undermines God's sovereignty in the purpose of Christ's advent. After all, the purpose of Jesus becoming fully man was so all of creation could relate to God through His Son. That being said, Jesus was a baby, a toddler, a little boy, a teenager, and a young man before He launched His earthly role as the Messiah. Meanwhile, He didn't raise Himself; He was mothered by an amazing young woman whose life is an example of extraordinary faith in the midst of great challenge and difficult times.

Over the centuries, wouldn't it have been helpful to the spiritual development of women and mothers if attention had been given to what God saw in Mary so they, too, could seek to grow and mature as Mary did? By closely examining Mary in her role in the greatest story ever told, we will understand why she was the greatest mother who ever lived.

> By closely examining Mary in her role in the greatest story ever told, we will understand why she was the greatest mother who ever lived.

God, consistent with His character, was intentional in selecting Mary as the mother of His only begotten Son. He could have chosen any woman at any moment in history. He could have selected an older woman with a greater heritage. He could have made her story one filled with ease, glory, and earthly riches. God knew if He did that, however, few women would relate, and it would put mothers on a track that did not reflect His heart or the life He longed for them to embrace. Instead, He selected a young teenager, an unmarried girl, to mother His child. How amazing is that?

Aren't you curious about what God saw in her? Have you ever wondered, as I have, *What is the other part of this story that He wants us to know?* Yes, there is more to the Mary story, and God does want us to know more about who she is and what she believed. By getting a glimpse of His heart for Mary, women and mothers will be encouraged, challenged, and inspired to live out the same faith-filled, gutsy devotion that Mary's journey called forth from her.

In this book, you will discover the intimacy with which God longs to participate in the life of a mother. Whether you are a mom and your relationship with your children is a prized treasure, or you're not a mother and your relationship with your mom has been a shaping force in your life, you will walk away with an insight into the gentleness of God toward us as His daughters.

Over the course of the next seventeen chapters, you will see how each scripture connected to Mary, the mother of Jesus, contains a truth that can deepen your faith. The Bible passages that so marvelously share her life will be joined by real-life stories from women just like you. There are plenty of stories about modern-day moms too. It felt right and good to couple our learning about Mary with examples from contemporary, every-day mothers. Every mom knows that when you're in the thick of it, it's not always a storybook experience. I'm sure Mary felt that same way at times! I want us to see the very real person who was the mother of Jesus in hopes that it will shed the light of truth on your own motherhood journey and bless mothers across generations.

But it only starts there. Another hope I have is that it will bless *all* women who need to be reminded of the enormity of God when life's overwhelming moments arise. Most likely, peering into the dynamic relationship between Mary and Jesus will also remind you of your own mom and the history there—both the good and the bad. Has it ever dawned on you that God sent your mother on a risky journey when He gave her the gift of you? There is freedom to be found in understanding your relationship to your mom through the lens of God's intentions. Above all,

> Mary's life will remind us that there are no accidents in God's divine plan for His daughters.

my hope is that Mary's life will remind us that there are no accidents in God's divine plan for His daughters and for those who are mothers. He longs to do in our lives the same things Mary invited Him to do in hers.

Mary's life is a canvas that allows us to watch God paint the picture of His character in her. We see a young woman who becomes fully authentic in the moment in which she is placed. She feels; she thinks; she questions. She is under the scrutiny of other women and knows that few will believe her about Jesus' divine conception. She is perplexed at her son's disappearance after the Feast of the Passover, and we see her experience deep anguish at the cross. Simply put, Mary is a deep woman who will encounter the same challenges other Jewish women of her day will face. Being the mother of a perfect child does not mean her journey will be free of sorrow, pain, or angst. It simply means she will have to rely on the same faith every woman needs in order to complete her motherhood expedition with peace and hope.

I invite you to walk this path with me. I want you to know Mary as an example of a woman who, as most mothers, wanted the best for her children and dared to trust God each step of the way. While Jesus would become her Savior too, He would first become her son. For all He would endure, what would never change was that Mary was His mom, and she loved Him that way. We can benefit from the perfection of Christ while embracing the mother-son rela-

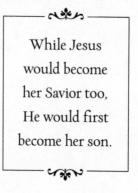

While Jesus would become her Savior too, He would first become her son.

tionship we see between Jesus and Mary and what it called out of her as a person of faith. Let us put fear aside so we can benefit from the wonderful role model God provided, not only for His Son, but also for all women who seek to obey God and for those who would follow in her steps of motherhood.

ONE

LOVE IN THE REARVIEW MIRROR

MARY KNEW GOD LOOKS AT THE HEART

*Now in the sixth month the angel Gabriel was
sent by God to a city of Galilee named Nazareth.*

—LUKE 1:26

L ife never goes as you plan it. Just as we were launching Taylor off to college, the kids' vehicle, an old SUV, bit the dust. Taylor and Tiffany had shared it through their high school years, and we were hoping to get another few years out of it. Unfortunately, it died a few days before we took Taylor to school.

Some dear friends saw our situation and wanted to bless us. They bought us a used car, one that had 30,000 miles on it. It was in great shape, and we were thrilled to get a car that worked well and that was not on its last leg. The only challenge for my family was that it was a stick shift, and I was the only one who knew how to drive a manual transmission.

Tiffany was beginning her senior year, and she would be attending a private school twenty-five miles from our home. We had been blessed for her to attend the school, because God had provided for her and Taylor's tuition. But now, with only two days before school was to start, she would have to learn how to drive the car.

The night before school began, Tiffany told me she did not

feel ready to drive a stick shift. I asked her what made her nervous about driving it. "I am scared I am going to conk out in the middle of the road, and people will honk at me," she said. "I do not want to deal with angry drivers."

I knew she was right. Having lived in South Florida my whole life, I was familiar with how impatient people could be. But I also knew that this was an opportunity for her to be stretched, so I did not want to let this moment pass. A thought dropped into my head that I know came from God.

"What if I follow you to school, so if you conk out and people get frustrated, they will honk at me? That way you get the driving practice, but I will be your rear guard and protect you from the hostile drivers," I said.

"What will I do in the afternoon when school is over?" Tiffany asked.

"I will be there waiting for you and follow you home," I replied.

"Okay, I can do that."

The next morning came, and off we went. We left early since we knew it might be an adventure. Sure enough, we weren't out of the neighborhood before Tiff conked out. I could see her eyes in her rearview mirror, and she had a panicked look on her face. She looked at me through the mirror, and I held up my thumb, giving her the sign that everything was okay. She smiled, started the car, and moved a little farther.

She conked out about five times that morning on the way to school. Every time she did, she would look back, and I would smile and give her a thumbs-up. She made it to school in one piece, with her mother right behind her the whole way. That afternoon I was waiting for her when she walked out of class, and we headed back home. She stalled a few times, but she was always protected from the impatient world because I was there.

This went on every morning and every afternoon for four days until we had time to take her to a driving course for her to practice. On Friday morning, she drove to school by herself without any problems and had the confidence to handle her travels from that day forward.

As I reflected on that experience, I was reminded of how God does the same thing with us if we let Him. He is always there, covering our backs, letting us know He is with us. That doesn't mean life always goes smoothly or is free of difficulties and challenges. What it does mean is that we can count on Him to never forsake us and to always love us. His love for us is intimate and sufficient for whatever trial we face. But we must be willing to love Him with all that we have and all that we are. That is what God loved about Mary: she had passionate love for Him.

Mary Was Chosen for Who She Was

When God selected Mary, He was looking for heart. God set out to find the precise woman who would give her heart to Him, completely and wholly. He wanted a woman with whom He could entrust His perfect Son. This was going to be no ordinary woman.

Or was it?

Mary was not a woman of status and means. Her family was probably considered "blue-collar" by the societal and cultural standards of her time. In Luke 1:48, she is described as "humble" (NASB), indicating a lowly position. She did not come from a place of influence and power. It appears that she was simple, pure, and young. Not a typical portrait for the mother of a king.

Yet God began the Jesus journey with the selection of the finest woman of that time. Theologians and historians believe that Mary was a young woman around the age of fourteen or fifteen. Since she had recently become engaged to Joseph, a carpenter, it is thought that she had just come into an age and body that the culture would define as a woman. While we can accept her youthfulness, it would be her heritage with which people would struggle.

> Mary was the unexpected selection in a journey that no one ever quite understood. For you see, the world was looking for a king to come from earthly royalty.

Even during that era, Mary did not fit the image of the mother of a king. Her background and simplistic life did not qualify her for the role. She was a Galilean, from an area known for its despicable ways. (How dare we believe that anything good could come from Nazareth! [See John 1:46.])

Mary was the unexpected selection in a journey that no one ever quite understood. For you see, the world was looking for a king to come from earthly royalty. God wanted His Son, the

King of kings, to come from a humble woman so that the entire world could relate.

Religious and political figures expected a king to be born of powerful, prestigious, and wealthy lineage so he could rule with authority and history behind him. God wanted King Jesus to come from a place where heritage and affluence could not buy Him His authority. God simply wanted His Son to embody the characteristics of His *own* heart. He wanted the world to recognize that His Son's value came from being God's Son. Nothing more. Nothing less.

God also wanted to instill in Mary that her value came from being God's daughter. This lesson is similar with children, but not exactly. They need to move through the world knowing that they are deeply connected to their mother, where their identity is rooted in something familiar and comfortable. The one difference is, they *also* need to anchor their identity in God, and put Him *first*. A mother is the facilitator and keeper of that identity formation.

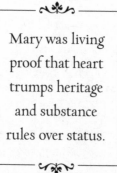

Mary was living proof that heart trumps heritage and substance rules over status.

Today's women struggle with the reality of their lives and their limitations. Too often they believe they are not good enough because they cannot provide all that the world says they need to give, including what they ought to give their children. Through Mary, God showed that what the *world* says is important isn't necessarily so; she was living proof that heart trumps heritage and substance rules over status.

Loving God Was Her Priority

Show me a woman who keeps her focus on Christ the way Mary did on her God, and I will show you someone who has 20/20 spiritual vision. This type of sight enabled Mary to maintain passion for her faith, purpose for her life, and a heart for her God. We see Mary giving God her life to do with as He desires. We see her "pondering" (Luke 1:29; 2:19 NASB), thinking her way through her motherhood moments. At the end of her son's life, we see her being steadfast and faithful in spite of her son's pain. Mary's success is that she quickly learned God was in the business of using the unlikeliest of people to reveal the most extraordinary truths of His heart and character.

> Mary's success is that she quickly learned God was in the business of using the unlikeliest of people to reveal the most extraordinary truths of His heart and character.

Mothers can see a turnaround in their parenting lives when they focus on God to define who they are. It is an amazing moment when women realize they do not have to live under the limitations of their past or their heritage.

I once had a mom come and speak to me before a conference we were doing for mothers and daughters. She seemed very anxious and nervous. I pulled her to the side to see if I could calm her down.

"Am I going to learn how to be a good mom at this conference?" she asked.

I told her that I thought she would learn many things, including the heart of being the mother God wanted her to be. I then asked her, "Are you worried you are not a good mom?"

The woman responded immediately, "I came from an abusive home, where my mom did not want me. It took me years to get up the courage to decide that I wanted to be a mother because I didn't want to repeat my background with my child."

"Have you parented differently than you were parented?" I asked.

Horrified at the question, the mother responded, "Absolutely!"

"How have you done it differently?" I gently questioned. I had a purpose in mind, but I needed her to list her strengths before I could intervene.

The mom began to immediately list all the ways she was parenting her daughter. It was clear she had worked very hard to give her daughter the emotional things she herself had needed as a child but had never received. As she began to wind down, I asked if I could point out something to her. She nodded.

"It is apparent you have worked very hard to mother your daughter differently than the way you were mothered. You have been intentional in loving her well, meeting her needs, and remembering the things that really matter. It seems as if the biggest enemy you presently have is the way you define yourself: you define yourself by your past instead of your God."

Her eyes looked intensely into mine. I could tell she was listening with her heart. I continued:

"God wants you to release your fear to Him. You cannot define your motherhood by how you were parented, but instead by the power of God to be what you need, when you need it. God will honor your heart's desire to raise your daughter in a manner that glorifies Him, but you must let go of your fears; they are getting in the way of you experiencing joy in motherhood."

This woman had heart. She had a passion for being a good mom. More than anything, she didn't want her daughter to ever go through what she had endured. And God would honor that desire.

Like this mom (and most others), I wanted to put my heart and soul into being a good mother. Because I'm a woman of deep passion and conviction, I do everything I do with all that I am. If I am wrong, I am 100 percent wrong. If I am right, I am passionately right. No lukewarm temperature on this mother's thermometer!

As a mom, I have made more than my share of mistakes. I have said things I never should have said, done things that experience would have me do differently, and reacted when I could have responded. In the midst of all my weaknesses and failures, however, the one thing my kids know is that I love them with everything I have. I believe that is one of the reasons they have been able to forgive me, be patient with me, and love me. They have known that my heart was always for them, in spite of my limitations.

I believe God selected Mary because she had a heart after His. She possessed a passion that status, lineage, and power could not touch. And she knew that God looked at her passion and love for Him. It would be for this reason alone that God would give her favor and blessing.

TWO

A WOMAN'S GREATEST BATTLE

MARY KNEW SHE COULDN'T EMBRACE HER
FEARS

*Then the angel said to her, "Do not be afraid,
Mary, for you have found favor with God."*

—LUKE 1:30

ear. It is the single greatest paralyzer of all time. It comes in many shapes and sizes. It is no respecter of persons, race, or status. It can cause big men to collapse, soldiers to crumble, and nations to retreat. It has sabotaged peace, prevented healing, and stirred division among families.

Fear is a dynamic that people embrace and give power to in their lives. It is the silent enemy of hope, reconciliation, and success. It undermines confidence and minimizes opportunities. Fear comes in forms both simple and complex. It respects no one, nor does it mind if it explodes in bigger-than-life fashion.

Gabriel had been in the angel business for quite a while and represented God's heart to His people. I have no doubt that Gabriel's words to Mary, warning her not to be fearful, came directly from God's mouth to Mary's ears. He knew that fright could easily take away her ability to hear of the miracle that she was getting ready to receive. Mary was a young Jewish maiden who had probably never thought of herself in any way worthy of a special glance; surprise and fear were going to be the emotions of the moment, and God was prepared for them.

"Do not be afraid" was not a request, but a command. When Gabriel declared that message to Mary, he was establishing the worthiness of God's protection and safety in her life. God was aware of her vulnerability in that moment, and He didn't want it to linger in her mind or heart. He wanted to remove her focus on her emotions and place it directly on Himself and His character.

This was significant, because Luke 1:29 tells us that she was greatly troubled. And why wouldn't she be? Here you have this humble Jewish maiden going about her business, just being a precious young woman who truly loved God. She was living an obedient, spiritually rich life, knowing that she had a future with a young man by the name of Joseph.

Since they were engaged, not married, Mary and her fiancé were still in the premarital phase of their relationship, getting to know each other, each learning how the other thought and felt.

So it is no wonder that Mary was troubled from the first moment the angel opened his mouth. She knew from Scripture that God had used angels throughout the ages to deliver special messages and important instructions. Mary had also heard the prophecies of Christ being born. Yet being the humble-minded person that she was, it never would have dawned on her that God would select *her* for this special occasion. She was a simple girl. What could Gabriel possibly want with her?

Mary Knew the Angel's Message Was Divine

The "Do not be afraid" came on the heels of a moment when Mary's mind was swirling with her knowledge of biblical history.

This command would be given to all the key players in the birth story of Christ. It was such an eternity-impacting event that no one was prepared to be a part of the moment. But that did not negate the fact that God was in charge and that He had selected the people He wanted to carry out His eternal plan.

God would not allow fear to sabotage His hope for eternity and the salvation of humanity. This is why He waited until Mary was at the right age in history to implement hope for all of us. He knew that a strong foundation had been laid within her about who He was so that in that very frightening moment, she would trust Him to be true to whatever He told her. Fear was one of Mary's natural human responses to which all people can relate. Isn't fear a normal reaction to the unknown and the unexpected?

Every mother has encountered fear. Whether it is a pregnant mom awaiting the impending birth, a birth mother giving up her baby for adoption, or an adoptive mother waiting for the adopted child to arrive, she is anxious because she has no control over whether her heart will be blessed or broken. I could go on for pages recounting the fears that fill the hearts of women everywhere—marriage, career, family, faith. Fear surfaces when we recognize that life may not go as we planned. Will we be able to cope or function if the carpet gets pulled out from under our world?

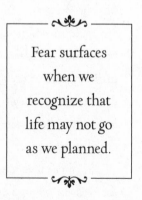

Fear surfaces when we recognize that life may not go as we planned.

Over the years, much of my professional attention has focused on parenting, family relationships, and motherhood. I have had the wonderful pleasure of observing, listening, teaching, coaching, and mentoring moms. I have worked with mothers who long to be the best they can be for their children, from the crib to adulthood. I have also picked up on several themes that seem to span age, experience, education, and socioeconomic levels. One theme in particular has done the most damage: fear.

As I've listened to their concerns, a major fear issue surfaces for most women and most aspiring mothers—that they would carry on the less desirable legacies of their own mothers. Several women have grown up in homes where their mothers looked good on the outside but had been emotionally empty and unavailable to them as children. Fits of rage, lack of nurturing, and critical comments were some of the experiences these women had personally encountered as kids.

This kind of environment deeply impacted these women's confidence levels when it came to living differently and doing things differently with their own children. It was affecting the way they managed their own kids now. I have seen an epidemic of mothers frightened to exhibit strength with their small children because they see *their* mothers come out in them when they get strong. Fearing they will do what was done to them, they back down from the preschooler, who then learns that he or she is in charge. Can you say, "Formula for creating a monster"?

Strong-willed children in particular need moms who are focused on what their children need, not on how they themselves were raised. When a mother can get out from underneath the fear of repeating the past and stay present with the needs of the moment, her child will most likely be parented in a manner that will serve him or her well. Fear of the past is holding many moms and kids hostage to an environment where the child is in control, which is the worst thing that can happen to a kid.

Every child needs to know that someone bigger is in charge. When the mom and dad assume their proper roles, it reduces anxiety, creates security, and promotes creativity. When moms live fearfully, however, their children suffer. They become increasingly out of control, which will impact them socially and academically. Iron-willed children will become very manipulative and obnoxious. Introspective children will take on fear-based qualities, including refusal to try new experiences, fear of relationships, and difficulty with trust. The bottom line is that no one wins!

> Every child needs to know that someone bigger is in charge.

All of these issues can surface simply because a mom is scared. How sad is that? These moms lie awake at night, worrying about the job they are doing as mothers. The longer that fear is allowed to linger, the greater the guilt that is produced as a result.

Let me give you an example. A mom goes to the grocery store with her two-year-old. Immediately the child grabs something off a shelf. Though Mom tells him he can't do that, she lets him hold the object, thinking it will pacify him. A few minutes later, he tosses the old item and grabs for another. Mom steps in and says no, but he immediately begins to scream at the top of his lungs, melting down in the middle of the store. Mom is embarrassed and angry at the same time. In order for her to manage the discomfort of the moment and calm the situation, she gives in. Unfortunately, she loses more than a battle. She loses her confidence.

Remembering the trauma of her own experience and probably blowing this most recent one with her own child out of proportion, she caves in to her shame. She becomes overly affectionate with her little boy, even apologizing for what she has done. He receives a mixed message, and once again, both the child and the mother lose. And the next time this event takes place, the stakes will get higher, and the child's tyranny will be more difficult to manage.

> We become like horses on a racetrack, our blinders allowing us only to see our fear of what *could* be instead of what God has already said is true about us.

Fear does that to moms, dads, bosses, employees, and anyone else who has breath in their bodies. However, it seems to especially impact Christians. Being fearful alters God's definition of us. We become like horses on a racetrack, our blinders allowing us only to see our fear of what *could* be instead of what God has already said is true about us.

Children need mothers who are not scared of themselves or their past. Wisdom says it is good to learn from our past experiences. However, that does not include having to live it out again. Children need the security of knowing that their moms are big enough to handle them and outlast them.

God Is Bigger than Anything You Fear

Several years ago, I had a mom bring her four-year-old daughter to my office. This mother was raising her child alone, without a support system, and seemed to be completely overwhelmed by her little girl. It was evident in the first two minutes that the child was also out of control.

I asked this mom if she let her little girl ignore her when she gave her instructions. She replied, "I tell her to obey me, and she doesn't listen!"

"What do you do with her after she has ignored you?" I asked.

"I tell her again," responded the mother. "I get frustrated and end up yelling at her. Then I feel bad."

I asked for a few more points of clarification, and it was soon obvious that the child had her mother's number. This behavior had begun before the yelling had taken place, but had only escalated since that time.

With the child in my office, I asked the mom if she wanted to practice making the little girl mind. She heartily agreed it was a great idea. Her opinion changed quickly, however, when the environment became stressful.

During our first few minutes together, this mom had allowed her daughter to roam throughout my office, opening cabinets that I would ask her to shut. When I asked the mother to have the girl come sit next to her on the couch, the little girl pretended to ignore her mother. I instructed the mom to tell her daughter that if she did not come and sit on the couch right now, she would have to go in time-out. The mom complied. The child ignored.

At this point, the mom gave me a *What do we do now?* look. "Go take your little girl by the hand and lead her to the corner," I said. "Tell her she will stand in the corner for four minutes. Once she has done that, she can come and sit with you on the couch."

Getting this little girl to the corner was like trying to drag an elephant by the tail. The kicking and screaming began at decibels I hadn't heard since the Fourth of July. The mom literally picked her up and plopped her in the corner; all the while the child was wailing.

> This isn't about you making her happy; this is about you making her behave.

The mom looked at me with horror. "She doesn't like this very much."

"You are right," I said. "But this isn't about you making her happy; this is about you making her behave."

I continued my education process with this mom over screams that sounded as if the child were being beaten to death. The mom needed encouragement, so I offered to take my turn with the child in the corner because she was still kicking and screaming.

I told the little girl that for every minute she screamed, she added a minute to her corner time. I literally held the child in the corner and calmly repeated to her that it was her choice to have to do things this way, and when she wanted out of the corner, she could make a different choice. Meanwhile, the mom was sitting on the couch, exhausted and amazed at the same time.

For more than thirty minutes, this little girl screamed. Eventually, the mom (with a little help from the therapist) out-lasted her. When the little girl finally broke, I bent down and told her that she had just made a really good choice and that I was glad she didn't have to stand in the corner anymore. That precious little whimpering girl reached out her arms and placed them around my neck. She held on tight to me for the longest time. I could feel her little body begin to relax and settle down. She then went over and sat in her mother's lap.

I never had issues with that child disobeying in my office again. The mother became one of my best students because she could see how important it was to the little girl for her to be strong and confident when she was parenting her.

A mother's fear can cripple a child's sense of well-being. Second Timothy 1:7 says, "God has not given us a spirit of fear, but of power and of love and of a sound mind." Maybe fear is the reason so many moms feel like they are losing their minds.

God's heart for women is to recognize that He understands the journey they are taking, and they need not be afraid. He makes our children and loves them more than life itself. He proved that through the birth and death of His own son, Jesus Christ. Isn't the same God who told Mary not to fear worthy of our obedience to trust Him also? You know it. And so did Mary.

> "God has not given us a spirit of fear, but of power and of love and of a sound mind."
>
> —2 Timothy 1:7

THREE

THERE ARE NO ACCIDENTS

MARY KNEW GOD AS MASTER DESIGNER

*"You will be with child and give birth to a son,
and you are to give him the name Jesus. He will be
great and will be called the Son of the Most High."*

—LUKE 1:31–32 NIV

We had just completed our first Kingdom Princess conference. I was both exhilarated and exhausted from a day that had exceeded my greatest expectations. The Kingdom Princess event was an opportunity for mothers and daughters to strengthen their relationships with each other. As I watched them leaving the event arm in arm, my heart was filled with gratitude and awe.

I felt a touch on my shoulder. As I looked up, a woman in her late thirties stood staring at me, tears streaming down her face. Worried that she was in some form of emotional pain, I asked her if she was all right. "Catherine, my tears are of joy, not pain. God healed me today. Thank you so much for creating this ministry."

I quickly told her that Kingdom Princess was God's idea and that I simply had the privilege of being a part of what God was doing. Curiosity, though, got the best of me. "Do you mind if I ask what got healed today?"

"For ten and a half years, I have struggled to be a mom to my stepdaughter. Her mother died when she was a year and a half old, and I have been raising her ever since her mother's death. Over the years, I have struggled with guilt and shame because I thought I was the wrong mother for her. We are so different from each other, and all this time I thought it was a mistake that I was her mom."

By this time, the tears were pouring from her eyes. Yet there was a steady confidence in her voice and a smile on her face. She continued.

"Today I learned that before the beginning of time, God picked me to be her mom, and her to be my daughter. It has been no accident that we were put together. For the first time in my life, I am comfortable in my skin and know that I am exactly what she needs in a mom. I simply have to rest in the truth that God put us together!"

Little did we know that she would be the first of many mothers who would be impacted by a simple scriptural truth.

Each Woman Has a Unique Plan

Mary, too, learned that God is sovereign in His selection of our children. This was an important lesson that God taught her at the beginning of her motherhood journey. He knew what lay ahead for Mary, and for her to be able to endure the trials and suffering of her firstborn child, she would have to know that God was in charge and that there were absolutely no accidents in her role as the mother of Jesus. Have you ever considered that God's selection of you for *your* mother was a divine appointment? Would you reconfigure your thinking about your experiences growing up, knowing that God has an eternal intention built into that relationship?

There had to be moments in Mary's humanness when she wondered why God had selected her. Because she was humble and knew herself so well, she never would have viewed herself as worthy. She could easily have thought that an older, wiser, more mature woman, one of means and standing, would have been better qualified for the privilege of being Jesus' mother.

> Have you ever considered that God's selection of you for *your* mother was a divine appointment?

No doubt, when Mary was faced with the uniqueness of Jesus or the unexplainable miracle of His birth, she felt lonely or frustrated by the inability to explain heavenly things to human hearts. What she did have, however, was the knowledge and experience of an angel telling her that she was the precise maiden God had selected throughout all of time to be the mother of our Savior. That moment would be one of many that she would ponder again and again.

Jewish history had taught her the Scripture of old, and Mary knew that the God of Abraham, Isaac, and Jacob had been strong, sovereign, and powerful. She knew God as creator and recognized Him as faithful, loving, and holy. Since she believed in God's omnipotence, she could trust that He knew her weaknesses and strengths. Thus, Mary made a decision to trust God as the Master Designer. She decided to believe that one of her first tests of faith was to trust in His selection of her for Jesus' mom. No small task for a teenage Jewish maiden!

Trusting the Father is one of the greatest challenges for any mother or mother-to-be, something I learned when my husband, Neil, and I started the adoption process. From the moment we spoke to the attorneys, I knew I was entering a path of trust, where I had no control over who our little child would be. When Neil and I first met with an attorney, whose name was Tom, he asked if there were any specifics we wanted him to consider. I never thought I'd have a chance to influence anything—I was going into it with completely open hands. But since he asked, I figured I'd tell him everything we hoped for in finding a child to adopt. It's an understatement to say he was not prepared for what I told him.

"First of all, we would like a baby to come from a married couple," I told him.

He looked at me with great surprise. "Married couples do not give up their babies. Why is that important?"

"I would prefer to tell a child he was conceived in love but the marriage didn't work out rather than to tell him we don't know who his father is," I said.

"We would like a baby who comes from an older couple," I continued audaciously.

Tom gave me that same bewildered look. "And why is that?"

"I think older parents will really understand the permanence of their decision. Once I hold that baby, I don't intend to give it back!" I said with conviction. Tom wrote it down on his list, but I could tell he was surprised by my boldness.

I listed off the remaining criteria. "We also want the baby to have medium- to high-level intelligence [so he could understand the adoption issues], the mother to have no history of alcohol or drug abuse, and for the parents to be Christians." Needless to say, Tom had never encountered a person like me who walked into the adoption process with a wish list so ungrounded in reality.

He put his pen down and looked at me as if I had three heads. "This will never happen," he said.

I looked straight back at him and said, "You asked me what I wanted, so I told you. My mom always said that you don't have if you don't ask. If God wants us to have a child with these criteria, then He will make it happen. If He wants us to have another child whose situation is different from what I have listed, then He will give us peace about that child."

The attorney shook his head and said, "It is going to be about two years before a baby will come your way. There are eleven other couples ahead of you. I will stay in touch."

Neil and I left the office excited and peaceful that someday we would be parents. It was okay that it might take awhile. We at least had hope that our dream would come true. (We also left behind an attorney who probably thought we were out of touch with reality. Little did he know.)

Because we'd had trouble having children of our own, Neil and I had learned how to wait. Since Tom had told us it would be several years, we went on about our lives. It never dawned on us that God might have a different timeline from our attorney.

"Are you sitting down?" Tom asked, when he called three weeks later.

I quickly sat down and said, "Yes, I'm sitting."

"Last night I met with a woman who is in her late twenties, college educated, a Christian with no history of alcohol or drug abuse, who has just divorced the baby's father. Every criterion you listed is wrapped up in this baby, and I know this is supposed to be your child," said our attorney. "Come in tomorrow at 5:00 so we can begin the legal process."

The first few days after our news were surreal. We had waited for years for this moment to come, and when it did, it was more than we could have anticipated. God had given us a miracle, and we would name that miracle, our son, Taylor.

Total Dependency Requires Total Trust

That experience would be the beginning of my dependency as a mom. There would be times of trial that would come in my early life as a mother when I would wonder if I had made a mistake in adopting Taylor. Not because of him and who he was, but because I felt so inadequate at times to handle the complications of his life. But every time I questioned my role as his mom, God would take me back to the meeting in the attorney's office when I listed my criteria. In His gentle way, God would remind me that He was the one who had given me the list and that I was the exact one He had chosen to be Taylor's mom.

Fourteen months after Taylor was born, I gave birth to Tiffany. It was a difficult pregnancy, and I nearly died in childbirth. Fortunately, she was healthy and wonderful, another miracle in our lives. How quickly we went from famine to feast.

Throughout my pregnancy, I was confused about the timing of this new baby. While I was overwhelmed with excitement, I could not figure out God's timing. I was curious as to why He'd allowed me to conceive when Taylor was so little. Why hadn't He given me more one-on-one time with Taylor, especially since I thought adopted children needed extra time in bonding? Yet I wanted my little girl so much that I had no qualms about her arrival.

Fortunately, God didn't ask me my opinion about His timing of my children's entries into the Hickem family.

A few months after Tiffany was born, overwhelmed by caring for two babies at once, I asked God again *why* He'd had them born so close together. I will never forget His response.

"Cathy, they are going to need each other in ways I cannot explain to you now. Because I've placed them in each other's life so young, they will never have a memory of what life was like without each other. You simply have to trust Me!"

While my body was still dragging, my heart became peaceful that God was in charge. It was such a comfort because my exhausted body and mind could hold on to the hope that there was a purpose to the 24/7 "feed them–change them–nap them–love them" chaos I was in!

I rested knowing that God had selected me to be Taylor and Tiffany's mom, regardless of whether I was the birth mother or not. And while I'm on the subject, parents who adopt can take heart knowing that even though they didn't physically create their children, God has always known that they would usher them through this life. His plan always accounted for it, and He has fully equipped adopting parents to be uniquely suited to their children's needs. But that doesn't for a second mean that it will be a cakewalk!

Today's first-time moms think they can control a lot of the details of their children's lives. That fantasy usually lasts about five minutes into labor, because that is when they realize how little control they have. They cannot influence conception (most women think they can), predict a child's personality type, or anticipate the trials and difficulties their children will encounter. Mothers are forced to cope with circumstances that are beyond their control and discover that they are in over their heads from the first day of birth.

Moms also learn very quickly that their children are full of surprises and fascinating mysteries. Trying to wrap their heads around their kids seems to become every mother's main goal. All of these out-of-control characteristics are perfectly designed by our heavenly Father.

When children are born, they are relatively simple to care for. Feed them, change them, wash them, hold them, and love them. For the most part, they are predictable.

As they grow, the pattern of predictability goes out the window. Their personalities form, they verbalize opinions, and they evolve with minds of their own. Diapers and sleepless nights become fond memories.

The growth and development of our kids can bring surprise, discomfort, and frustration to mothers, especially if preconceived expectations are unfulfilled.

My friend Nancie Carmichael was the mother of four sons when she and her husband, Bill, felt led to adopt a little girl from overseas. The whole family was excited about the new addition to their family.

Let me tell you about my friend Nancie. She is to motherhood what Norman Rockwell was to painting. She is the type of mom every person wished he or she had. She has a wonderful relationship with her children and has a great partnership with Bill. She is a real woman with a real heart for God.

> The growth and development of our kids can bring surprise, discomfort, and frustration to mothers, especially if preconceived expectations are unfulfilled.

When it came time for Amie to arrive in their family, Nancie had it all planned. Amie would like the color pink, want bows in her hair, play with dolls, and love frilly dresses. At least that is what Nancie planned. Guess who got surprised?

Amie *didn't* like pink, dolls, bows, or frilly dresses. She liked athletics and doing the things her brothers did. She was the opposite of everything Nancie had imagined. What a jolt to Nancie's heart! She felt betrayed.

As Nancie tells the story, she talks about how God used her expectations, frustrations, disappointment, and fear to teach her more about Him. This journey would be the catalyst God would use to show Nancie what trusting Him really looked like. It would also be His vehicle to teach her how to love Amie unconditionally. The journey would demonstrate to Nancie over and over again that He had given her the exact daughter He wanted her to love. There had been no mistakes.

I think we go into motherhood altruistically. We want to make a difference by creating a life that positively impacts the world. We think that because they are our kids, we will know everything there is to know about them and that nothing will surprise us. We are confident that we can fix it all, know it all, and love them enough to make their lives happy and complete. I believe that a mother's determined heart to "be it all" must bring a snicker from God as He watches us being humbled by the smallest of people.

In my own journey, I believe God has used my kids as sandpaper to refine the rough edges and bumpy places in my life. Nothing grabs our hearts like our kids. And God designed it just that way.

Who Teaches Whom?

My children have been my greatest teachers. God has used them to strengthen my faith, humble my pride, and inspire me to believe the impossible and pray like there's no tomorrow. Their idiosyncrasies were probably designed for my behalf. Would they make me crazy, or would they make me more dependent? I think God had "dependent" in mind.

Mary had no idea, when she agreed to obey the Lord, all that obedience would entail. She would be given a child to rear that no one would ever fully comprehend. She would parent a little boy who would become the Savior of the world, yet those closest to her would not recognize or appreciate the truth of His identity. As a result, she would constantly be placed in a position requiring her to trust God to empower her for a task that no one in the world would ever repeat. Her closest companions would question her son's heritage (out-of-wedlock birth), His unusual compliance, His extreme intelligence, and His alarming maturity. And though, unlike the rest of us moms, she wouldn't have to encounter issues involving typical teenage temperament and identity crisis, her journey would involve a child so atypical compared to all the other kids that she would have to fully depend on the God who had selected her.

My children have been my greatest teachers.

Isaiah 49:1 tells us that God knows us by name, and Psalm 139 says that He knit us together in our mothers' wombs. When I read these passages, I see God holding an infant in His hands. Looking over the course of a baby's life, He places within it all the things the baby will need to become the full creation of His beauty. He selects the eye color, personality type, gifts, parents, body type, and birth date. There are no accidents in His design. Each baby is complete in every way, according to His plan for the little child's life.

In Luke 1:31 we see that God had a specific child in mind for Mary. We all know that this was no ordinary child, so it is easy for us to explain and justify the attention given to Jesus and

His mother. We must remember, however, that God is equally attentive to all children born, because they, too, are His.

Because we are born in the heart of God before we are born in the wombs of our mothers, we must recognize that our lineage begins with Him. Our definition of ourselves must not come from our earthly parents. While I may have my father's hair, my mother's eyes, and my aunt's temperament, those are simply threads that God has woven together to tie me to my earthly family.

> Because we are born in the heart of God before we are born in the wombs of our mothers, we must recognize that our lineage begins with Him.

People have always wondered when adopted children look like their adoptive parents. But if we believe that we begin in the arms of God, then doesn't it make sense that God creates each child to favor the very family that will raise him or her as their own?

The result of life beginning with the Master Designer means each child is born of royal heritage. Each person's gene pool carries within it a lineage of nobility. How powerful it is to realize that each of us begins as royalty!

The power of that royal lineage continually reminds children of their secret heritage, though they may not understand it. As parents, we must choose to see our children the way God does—as His offspring too. All along God wants us to remain in the royal family, but because He loves us so much, He wants us to *choose* to love Him. It is called *freedom* and *honor*, and He knew from the start that forced love was not really love at all. This is something He longs for our children to understand and see embodied by us. But we are God's children too! If you are reading this sentence right now, God wants you to know your heritage in Him so you can live in that assurance before everyone.

When a mother can embrace the belief that God created her and designed her children, she can then trust God to watch over the rest of her journey to parent them. Confidence grows and burdens are lifted when mothers catch a bigger picture of their kids' lives.

Especially important to a child's self-worth is the confidence that a mother has in her God. When a child can sense that a mother knows in the deepest place of her heart that God selected her to be his or her mom, it communicates a power-ful sense of strength and confidence to the child, bonding child to parent. Just as two scrambled eggs can never be unscrambled, a mother and child who are intertwined in God's heart will never separate.

> Just as two scrambled eggs can never be unscrambled, a mother and child who are intertwined in God's heart will never separate.

Like Mary, who was with Christ at the cross, a godly mom will remain connected to her child throughout the journey of life. If she is able to rest in God's sovereignty in the selection of her kids and who God created them to be, then she can be about the business of know-ing God in other ways. She will be able to rest in the midst of difficulties, surprises, and U-turns because she will know that God, being the Master Creator, is never surprised by any of His creations. It is simply a mom's job to trust Him to help her walk through each moment with them.

FOUR

THE TRUE MEANING OF QUESTIONS

MARY KNEW SHE COULD ASK GOD QUESTIONS

Then Mary said to the angel, "How can this be, since I do not know a man?"

—LUKE 1:34

There is an old adage that says, "No question is a stupid question." You might argue with that line of thinking, given some of the questions you have heard people ask over the years. The point of the proverb is that a question indicates a desire to know something more than what is known.

Some of us may remember times when we asked questions to avoid dealing with issues, to delay a teacher or professor, or to enhance our position on a particular argument. Often a good attorney will pose a series of questions to a jury during a trial because he or she wants to create doubt among them. Thus, questions serve many purposes.

It has often been considered negative for people to ask questions of God because it can be perceived as mistrusting Him. Many Christians also mistake questioning God for arrogance because they believe that one should never challenge God on any of His decisions or actions. However, this attitude is not reflective of biblical truth or sound parenting.

Mary's question to the angel was an honest response to having her world turned upside down. She had just been told that her life was going to begin with a sex scandal even though she had never before been sexual. The query recognized the facts of the moment, not her doubt in her God.

Mary's overwhelming appointment as mother of the Savior of the world takes on a very human characteristic when we see her asking God's messenger a *question*. How freeing is that for all of us who have stared uncertainty in the face and wondered what God was up to?

> Mary's question to the angel was an honest response to having her world turned upside down.

Mary's inquiry was an earnest attempt for this young teenager to get her hands around her world. She so wanted to grasp all that was being said because she seemed to have a glimpse of the importance of the message being delivered. We see a woman trying to understand a divine call from limited, human perspective. She was young, but she was old enough to know that she did not have all the pieces to put together the puzzle that was being laid before her.

Although Mary did not initially understand the divine message, she knew it had to be extremely important because it was not every day that an angel personally delivered a word from God. She also sensed that the moment was not about her, but about her God. Knowing He had ordained that moment in time, she wanted to be sure that she internalized as much as possible so she would not get in the way of what God was trying to accomplish.

The Gift of Mary's Questions

I must tell you that I am so grateful that Mary asked God questions. She was able to quickly comprehend the situation she was in and authentically put her concerns before God. The blessing for us in this exchange is that she gives all people permission to throw the tough questions at the Father. She also shows us how real her relationship was with God.

As a psychotherapist, I sit with many people who are in various forms of crises. I always know there is a major problem when there is an overly compliant person in a relationship. When one person never challenges, questions, or explores the why, where, when, or how of a relationship, I know the couple is in big trouble.

Some people think that total compliance is an act of love and submission. I see it more as a dysfunction, however, because there is no way that one person in a relationship is going to have all the correct answers. When an individual never challenges or questions anything, then it tells me that complacency or fear has set in and passion and interest have left.

It is healthy for people to discuss and question. Great communication takes place when we are free to process our thoughts and feelings without judgment or condemnation. It is also significant

> When an individual never challenges or questions anything, then it tells me that complacency or fear has set in and passion and interest have left.

when a person has the opportunity to question without people taking it personally.

My son, Taylor, is a natural questioner. For the first ten years of his life, I didn't understand the purpose of his questions. Sometimes I thought he was just being obnoxious, and I would find myself really annoyed by this tendency.

As I began to explore the different personality types, however, I realized that being a questioner was his natural bent. He truly needed additional information in order to process his thoughts and feelings. Once I grasped this behavior as a part of who God had created Taylor to be, I became more supportive of that part of him. It enhanced our relationship immensely because it said to him that I understood and respected his needs.

Another observation I have made over the years is that children who ask a lot of questions are usually very bright. Their desire to understand will serve them well in their academic journeys and other areas of their lives because it says that they are teachable, open, and willing to grow.

Most important, when questions can be asked of people in authority, it says volumes about the person in submission. Let me further explain.

Too often in work situations, employees will not ask the boss a question for fear that they may appear vulnerable and unworthy of hire. As a result, they will overcompensate or dance around the issue, hiding their ignorance. Eventually, though, their refusal to inquire catches up with them, and the consequences are usually worse than if they had been forthright with their question or lack of understanding.

Whether it is a child, a spouse, an employee, or a follower of Jesus, the freedom to ask questions speaks volumes about the safety and trust the person feels with the one questioned. When people have the security to reveal their vulnerability, they are far more likely to accomplish the goals before them. Simply put, they do not have to be concerned with self-preservation. They are allowed to stay focused on the task at hand, which will further allow them to fulfill their purpose with greater clarity, hope, and success.

We have always told our kids that we want to be the ones they come to with the difficult questions. We knew that if they felt safe enough to ask us the hard questions, then it would communicate that we had created the right environment for our kids to trust us.

Permission to Struggle

Over the years, I have heard many parents say they want their kids to come to them with their questions. Yet, when the difficult moments arise, they send the opposite message.

In my first job out of graduate school, I worked at a children's therapy clinic. I saw children from all different types of backgrounds with a multitude of problems and issues. It was like working the MASH unit in the military.

One of the positions that came open was the opportunity to work with kids who were patients at a pediatric tumor clinic. In the early '80s, the success rate for these serious childhood diseases was not as high as it is today. I thought it would help me grow as a therapist if I tackled the most challenging problem a parent could face.

My first patient was an eight-year-old girl whom I will call Sarah. She had leukemia and had been undergoing treatment for more than a year. She had been referred to me because she was so angry. She was acting out in the hospital, and the staff thought she could benefit from speaking with someone.

I saw the mother first. She told me that Sarah didn't know her condition was as bad as it was. I gently questioned her as to whether or not Sarah might know more than she thought. "Absolutely not," said the mom. "I told her that she could ask me anything and I would tell her the truth. But she hasn't asked me."

I asked the mom if I could spend some time with Sarah by myself, and she said it would be fine. The mother went out to the waiting room, and Sarah came in. What happened next was profound.

Sarah shut the door behind her. I had sat down in my chair and was looking at her as she walked across the room toward me. "Can I ask you a question?" she asked me directly, looking into my eyes.

"You can ask me anything you want," I said.

"Can we talk about dying? My mom can't handle it when I bring it up, but I need to talk about it. Can you handle it?" she asked me, with her eyes piercing into mine like a laser beam.

"Sarah, we can talk about any part of dying you want. Where do you want to start?" I asked.

Sarah proceeded to talk about what she thought heaven was

like and how at night she had bad dreams because she would be separated from all the people she knew and loved.

Heavy issues, heavy hearts. Sarah is like so many kids who learned early on what her mom could and could not handle. My introduction into the world of dying children was powerful and humbling. I learned how hard children fight to protect their parents from painful things. I watched children hold on beyond human limits so their parents could have more time to let them go. I learned that kids know when it is safe to be real and vulnerable with their doubts, their fears, and their questions.

> Kids know when it is safe to be real and vulnerable with their doubts, their fears, and their questions.

I have worked in Christian schools over the years, and what I have observed seems to be congruent with what other professionals have seen. Many kids who have come from Christian homes have learned that asking their parents difficult questions only creates havoc for them personally. Questions raise suspicion, cause doubt, and intensify control, none of which a teenager wants in his or her life.

As a result, the teen learns which questions to never ask, which ones are safe, and which ones the parents want to hear. This forces the child to develop a double life, which becomes a pattern for hypocrisy. While teens may appear to enjoy the so-called freedom that comes with this deception, in their hearts they wish they could actually be real and vulnerable. Deep inside they know that they do not have the wisdom they need to navigate the waters of adolescence. Yet they have learned they have nowhere to turn.

I know a fourteen-year-old who once asked his mother a sexual question that came from a natural place of curiosity, but that would make most people blush. Since it was a female-related question, it was logical that he would turn to his mom. After she had answered him as best she knew how, the teen said to her, "Thanks, Mom!"

"For what?" she said.

Her son responded, "You didn't blink when I asked the question."

God doesn't blink when we ask Him questions either, regardless of how raw or seemingly inappropriate they may be. Our willingness to throw difficult challenges at Him is an opportunity for us to see His faithfulness and power in our lives. Our inquiries are also an indication of our openness to being vulnerable and intimate with Him. The more we are willing to be real and honest with God, the more we will see God do the impossible in our lives.

> God doesn't blink when we ask Him questions either, regardless of how raw or seemingly inappropriate they may be.

Mary's question to the angel revealed her trust in the Father. Inquisitiveness was an important virtue in Mary because she would be the role model for Christ in His relationship with His Father. He questioned the rabbis; He questioned the established religious powers; He even questioned the

Father in His time of need. Where do you think He learned to do that?

On the cross, in the final moments of His suffering, Jesus asked, "My God, My God, why have You forsaken Me?" (Matthew 27:46). In that one brief moment, Jesus gave all of humankind permission to question God on the difficult moments of life. How powerful and freeing it is to know that we can reveal our deepest struggles to our God without fear.

For us to be the kind of parents our children deserve, we get to practice as children with God. The easier we are able to take our questions to God, the easier it will be for our children to bring their questions to us. As trust grows between us and God, we will have a better ability to create an atmosphere of trust and safety for our own children to approach us with the hard questions in life. More than anything, God longs for moms to reflect authenticity to their children so that trust and respect will permeate their relationships.

IN OVER HER HEAD

MARY KNEW SHE COULD NOT PARENT JESUS
ON HER OWN

*And the angel answered and said to her, "The
Holy Spirit will come upon you, and the power of
the Highest will overshadow you; therefore, also,
that Holy One who is to be born will be called the
Son of God."*

—LUKE 1:35

M ary had just asked the angel the biggest question of her life. She had been told she was going to become the mother of the Son of God. In the moment of this revelation, Mary's question reveals her awareness of the task before her. It also reflects Mary's depth and insight to recognize she was going to need help to accomplish this ever-important responsibility.

God selected Mary because He could trust her with the responsibility of raising Jesus. In fact, it is safe to say that God had more confidence in Mary than she had in herself. He knew He could count on her to lean on Him for help because she recognized the awesome privilege with which she had been entrusted. While she didn't fully comprehend the journey, she knew it would not be ordinary.

The angel's response tells us that great parenting is going to require a supernatural element. No mother will have all the answers or wisdom to parent her children successfully. The job is too difficult, the children are too challenging, the culture is always changing, and the needs are too great for any mom to pull this off by herself. She must have help to fulfill the most emotionally intense relationship of her life.

Mary was probably hopeful that this supernatural interaction would be a sign of things to come. She must have felt some relief when the angel told her she would not be on her own to raise the one and only Son of God. She was smart enough to know how difficult it was to be a good mother in *any* case, but to be responsible for raising the King of kings was another story.

The angel's answer is one every mother in the world should embrace. When the angel told her, "The Holy Spirit will come over you, and the power of the Most High will overshadow you," he was giving all moms the key to parenting success: acknowledging God's presence. He is always with us. The question is, will we allow Him to be a part of the relationship?

Like Mary, all moms feel vulnerable at different moments in their mothering journey. We are often puzzled by our children's behavior, confused by their personalities, bewildered by their emerging thoughts, and scared of our increasing lack of control in their lives. Many times we find ourselves totally uncertain of who our children are and how we are to respond to the issues they face. Is there any wonder we need help?

Power Greater than Our Own

Being a mother is a very daunting experience. It is one you really never master because children change just about the time you figure them out. Thus, it is the wise mom who invites God to participate in her motherhood story.

When my son, Taylor, was ten years old, he developed a problem with solving math equations and spelling words correctly. I knew something was up because math had been his strongest academic area and he was typically a good speller.

> The key to parenting success: acknowledging God's presence.

After a week or two of trying to solve this problem on my own, I took him to our pediatrician, who immediately sent us to a pediatric ophthalmologist. The news was not encouraging. He sent us to a pediatric neurologist at a hospital about seventy-five miles away from our home. Needless to say, I was beginning to get nervous.

We arrived at our neurology appointment, and after a day of tests, the doctors asked to speak with me alone. "Mrs. Hickem, we need to admit Taylor for further testing. We have some concerns about what possibly might be the problem, but we cannot know for sure until we have done a thorough workup," said one doctor.

When I pressed them for further information as to what they were looking for, I was told that it could be anything from epilepsy to a brain tumor or a degenerative brain disease. Needless to say, I was stunned. I sat quietly and listened, trying to process all that they were saying. I was composed, thoughtful, and incredibly peaceful.

"Mrs. Hickem, do you understand what we just said?" asked the lead neurologist.

"Yes, I do," I said. "Why do you ask?"

"You are so calm that we wondered whether you have heard us." (I guess most moms had responded quite differently to such news, and my reaction had thrown them off.)

"I totally understand that what you just told me could be really life-changing for Taylor. In fact, I realize that what you said could even mean death. But what I know is that when we get to the end of man, we get to the beginning of God. It will be in Him that I trust for the outcome," I said to both physicians. The room was silent for a moment. We then went about the business of scheduling my son's hospital admission.

> When we get to the end of man, we get to the beginning of God.

I loaded Taylor into the car and headed home in the middle of late-Friday-afternoon traffic. The rain was falling harder than some hurricanes I had experienced, which only lengthened a lonely trip. Taylor had fallen asleep in the back of the van, which left me alone with my thoughts and feelings.

As the news started to sink in, I began to feel the emotions the doctors had expected earlier. I was completely aware of my helplessness to fix my son. I was even more aware of the risk of losing him.

I started to sob—and then, to pray.

"God, thank You for giving Taylor to us for the last ten years. Thank You for all You have taught us through him and all the wonderful ways You have created him. God, I am going to ask that You give me many more years with Taylor."

I wanted to end the prayer at this point, but I knew I had more to tell God. I didn't want to pray the next part of my prayer, but my heart would not rest until I did.

"God, I want Taylor to live a long time, but if You have another plan, then I am going to ask You to help me have a thankful heart and give me the grace to reflect You while we walk the journey," I prayed between my sobs. This was the most difficult prayer I had ever prayed, and I knew only God knew how the story would end. I was never more aware of my need for something stronger than I am to help me be the mom Taylor needed.

Days later, Taylor underwent three days of exhaustive testing. At the end of the last day, two of Taylor's doctors we had not yet met came to his hospital room. As they walked into the room, the chief pediatric neuro-ophthalmologist informed us there was nothing wrong with Taylor, but wanted to know if he and the other physician could pray over Taylor. Of course we agreed to this gracious offer. He went on to tell us that God had told him during Taylor's exam that prayer would correct the issues we were facing. From the day we left the hospital, Taylor never had another episode.

The Gift of God's Presence

Why did we go through this with Taylor? What was God trying to teach me as a mom? I think the lessons were many, but I especially believe God wanted me to deepen my trust in Him. Like Abraham with Isaac, I needed to be willing to relinquish my son to the Lord. God also wanted me to learn that the only way I could walk my motherhood journey well was to totally depend on Him.

Of course, this story is in the crisis category, but the lesson applies to the day-to-day experience of motherhood. I have prayed for wisdom on everything from when to start potty training to handling broken curfews. Nothing has been too big or too small for me to ask, all because God offers me what He offered Mary: His willingness to be the wisdom I need at any moment of my journey.

Like Mary, you and I must be willing to take the help that is offered. I have always seen God as a gentleman, one who never forces His way on us. He lovingly invites us to take Him up on His offer to be a part of our lives. The reason Mary was successful was that she never forgot the angel's message: "The Lord is with you" (Luke 1:28).

> The reason Mary was successful was that she never forgot the angel's message: "The Lord is with you."

Dependency requires trust. Many women I know struggle to trust God because of the wounds they have suffered from their own moms and dads, the men in their lives, or the disappointments they have experienced. If you are a mom and mistrust is an issue for you, then it can be passed down to your children.

At the end of the angel's message, he declared, "For nothing is impossible with God" (Luke 1:37 NIV). This would be his final declaration to Mary. It ended on a note of power and grandiosity. He wanted Mary to be assured of God's sovereignty and authority because the future would test her faith in every way as a mom. Letting her know up front how big God is would create a memory she could rely on in her future when things got tough. Can't you hear the conversations she would have with God regarding this verse?

What about you? Are you tired of trying to mother on your own? As a woman, are you tired of running your life on your own terms? It is never too late to change the way you look at God and how you mother your children. God is always looking for a woman who will let Him come in and redeem her past mistakes, heal her heart, and make a new future for her family.

SIX

THE POWER OF A SELFLESS LIFE

MARY KNEW HER LIFE WAS NOT HER OWN

*Then Mary said, "Behold the maidservant of the
Lord! Let it be to me according to your word."
And the angel departed from her.*

—LUKE 1:38

M ary's dreams of a quiet life with Joseph had flown out the window with the angel's pronouncement of her impending pregnancy. Now, here she stood, engaged and pregnant outside of wedlock: a condition that at worst could threaten her life, and at best could result in both a scandal in the village and a damaged reputation.

It wasn't enough that she would have to explain her condition to her family. She would also have to endure public scrutiny from those who knew her best, and live with the fact that most would never believe her regarding her encounter with the angel. Mary's divine destiny would not resonate with her Jewish family and friends with whom she lived because their King, they believed, was to come as royalty, not from humble beginnings such as hers.

Thus, in the process of assuming her new role, she began to realize that her life would be very different from the dreams and expectations she had embraced for herself. To trust God with this new journey would mean she would have to release her dreams to God and accept what He had for her. In this moment, she had to step outside of her wants and desires and embrace the unexpected. In other words, she had to trust.

Let's face it, as women we want what we want. Mothers might even have a double dose of this when you think about a child in a full-blown tantrum. We ladies can be a determined, diligent group of people, and if you ever bump into a crowd of moms united over a cause for the sake of their children—watch out! Trying to get a woman to let go of her ideals could be compared to trying to move an elephant with a feather.

Mothers have dreams for their children the moment they are placed in their arms. They mentally and emotionally prepare to do what they can to ensure that their children have every opportunity to succeed and be happy. These thoughts never go away and often become the focus of struggles between mother and her offspring as the child moves into adulthood.

> Trying to get a woman to let go of her ideals could be compared to trying to move an elephant with a feather.

Holding on to expectations has often been the death knell of parent–adult child relationships. Many times parents will lock into what they have wanted for their children all along, and any deviation from that dream or expectation will cause a gap in the connection between them. Misplaced expectations can create deep hurt, broken communication, and huge disappointment. More important, they can permanently damage the parent-child bond.

Moms and dads often have personal dreams and hopes that have gone unfulfilled. Children, regardless of age, rarely recognize either the fact that their parents ever had such dreams or that they may be living them out through their children. Most of the time, parents themselves lack awareness in this area and have never fully grieved what might have been.

As a result, it is easy to relate to Mary's situation. If Mary were your daughter, would you, as her mom, have been scared, sad, or overwhelmed by the series of events? Probably so. Not because you didn't trust God, but because you had spent her entire life believing it was going to look a certain way, only to find out there would be nothing predictable about your daughter's journey. Time would help you adapt and redirect your dreams.

Mary's age and her faith allowed her to quickly make a choice to trust God with her future and her life. Although it was not going to be what she thought, she knew that whatever God decided would be what was right for her. God knew He could count on her to see things from His perspective.

Mary Recognized God's Authority

Another significant reason we see Mary take her bold step of faith is because she knew God as her authority. This understanding of His role in her life would be paramount to her journey as the mother of the King. This is also where we see the richness of her faith heritage come alive.

One of the challenges in today's culture surrounds the issue of authority. If it is not handled well at home, then attitude problems will surface in children and teens that will affect them for the long term. There are certain seasons in childhood, adolescence, and young adult development when power and control issues will surface. In a healthy family, they will be transitory. Most children grow out of the "terrible twos" because it is a stage. When power struggles are handled inappropriately over the course of the child's life, however, resistance to authority will rear its ugly head as he or she progresses toward adulthood.

Mary understood that there was no better place to be than in a place of obedience to God's plan and will. Most young women would have run the other direction after reflecting on what the angel's message really meant. But not Mary. Her faith ran deep, and trust was a part of her earthly DNA. Her courageous act of submission reflected greatly on how she had been raised and the foundation upon which she was reared.

> Mary understood that there was no better place to be than in a place of obedience to God's plan and will.

I have always said that the first person I want to meet when I get to heaven is Mary's mother (after meeting God first, of course). Although she is never mentioned by name, we see her invisible presence in Mary's life and faith. Jewish maidens learned about the nature and character of God at the knees of their mothers. Daughters were not allowed to attend school, so most of their spiritual knowledge was gained through their significant female relationships inside the home. No doubt, for Mary to have the necessary confidence in God to declare such allegiance to Him, she had been taught well of His trustworthiness and faithfulness. What about your mom? Do you feel the invisible cords of strength and peace from her life to yours? Or, like most women, will you have to make some intentional choices to untangle some of the complicated knots and create new strands of beauty and strength for those around you?

Too often, today's moms do a great job of exposing their children to religious activities, but come up short in demonstrating and teaching the real dynamics of knowing God. We teach our kids *about* God, but fail to teach them to *know* God. Clearly, Mary knew God in a real and personal way.

> We teach our kids *about* God, but fail to teach them to *know* God.

When we know someone's character and heart, it frames what our questions will be. If we know someone to be true, honest, safe, and loving, questions indicating fear and doubt will not be the first thoughts we entertain. On the other hand, if we know someone to be sneaky, selfish, and prideful, we will be cynical about that individual's motives and begin the relationship with a guarded heart.

When we really know God, we can bypass the initial moments of skepticism. We may still question Him, but it will come from a place of wonder and honesty, not fear and punishment. Mary had clearly learned that He was worthy of her faith and allegiance. Regardless of what was to come (and it would be plenty), she could count on Him to be with her and see her through whatever she might face.

Life is always going to be more peaceful if we let go of our definition of what we want in exchange for what God has for us. As Mary's story unfolds, we will see that it only gets harder the older Jesus becomes. This is not an unusual place for parents to find themselves, especially as they move into their children's young adult years. Sometimes embracing the new direction our lives take is not easy.

Her Identity Was in Her God

My mother was the principal of a school for handicapped children for more than twenty years of her career. It was a job she found meaningful and fulfilling. The youngest a child could enter her school was five, and the oldest was twenty-one.

One day we were discussing her observations of the families of disabled children. She had always admired their tireless commitment to their children as well as their determination to pursue every avenue possible to improve their children's quality of life.

"One thing I have noticed is the difference between those parents whose children are born with a disability versus those whose children develop a disability after years of normality. It seems as if the parents who have to adjust their dreams after a disabled child is born have an easier time of moving on than those who saw the possibilities of what could be and will never know," said my mother. In other words, parents of a child who was born healthy but who was later in a life-changing accident or developed a chronic illness had a more difficult time coming to terms with their "new normal," and this was completely understandable.

When we take the approach that our life is not our own, we will reframe unexpected moments. We will find value and meaning no matter what happens to our children or to us. This does not mean it will always be easy. I think we can agree there was nothing easy about Mary's life. If she were here today, however, I have no doubt she would do it all over again.

My uncle Sonny was a wonderful man. He married in his thirties and his wife had their first child, John, at the age of thirty-seven. I noticed rather early that John was not as responsive as other babies I had been around. It would take awhile (in the '70s, diagnostic processes took longer) before we would know that John had cerebral palsy as well as mental retardation. Uncle Sonny and Aunt Pat worked faithfully to help John learn to walk and feed himself. While he never learned to talk, he did learn to communicate his basic needs and wants.

Seven years later, they had a little girl named Jessica. She was a cute little thing, but once again, something was not right. Cerebral palsy visited this family for the second time, along with a lower mental capacity. While Jessica's condition was less severe than her brother's, it still required intense attention and time.

Five years after Jessica was born, my aunt entered the hospital with what seemed to be severe flu or a gastrointestinal disorder. Unfortunately, she was diagnosed with one of the rarest cancers in the world and three months later died without ever returning home.

Shortly after my aunt's death, Neil and I went to visit my

uncle and his two children. He was now all alone, not only with their care, but also with maintaining a business. I knew he deeply missed Aunt Pat and noticed how quiet the house was, since the kids could not speak.

I marveled at his patience and gentleness. "Uncle Sonny, how do you do this?" I asked in wonder. His sweet, worn face turned to me and said, "Cathy, I am so blessed. I couldn't ask for anything more. God has given me so much, and every day He gives me the grace to make it through whatever the day brings." I have no doubt he meant every word he was saying. His life had always reflected character, faith, and integrity, and his walk was true to his talk.

He didn't ask for disabled children. He didn't ask to become a widower at forty-nine. He also didn't ask to get cancer himself and die at the age of fifty-four. Fortunately, he was able to make arrangements for his children's care with family members he knew would care for them in his absence. But up until the last moment of his life, he trusted God at every turn. The man who the world would say was cursed would argue that he was most blessed. All this was possible because he trusted God with his life.

When a person's identity is in his God, he will find the greatest peace and have the biggest impact. People with this kind of confidence let go of what they think their lives should look like and embrace what they have been given as an opportunity to be used of God for His purposes and not their own.

Dear friend, where does your confidence and identity come from? Is it your career? Your spouse? Your ability to keep all the plates spinning? Dear moms, how about you? I don't ask these questions to create guilt or shame—I'm as prone to lean on anything but God as the next person. Mary shows us a different way—that our value to God is not contingent on any one thing we do or don't do. He sees us as sparkling jewels because that's the only way He *can* see us. Why do we so rarely see ourselves the way God sees us?

> God sees us as sparkling jewels because that's the only way He *can* see us.

And, moms, we need to keep at the forefront of our thoughts that we need to see children from God's perspective. If your children are difficult and challenging, God thinks no less of them and He's trusted *you* enough to raise them. There will also be something God wants to do in your life that only your demanding children could teach. Isn't that why we are here? To know God? What better way than to let our children be our teachers.

SEVEN

SMART WOMEN KNOW THEY NEED OTHER WOMEN

MARY KNEW SHE NEEDED SUPPORT

Now Mary arose in those days and went into the hill country with haste, to a city of Judah, and entered the house of Zacharias and greeted Elizabeth.

—LUKE 1:39–40

G od was so good to share with us the significant con-nection between Mary and Elizabeth. It speaks volumes about the value He places on relationships and His understanding of a woman's need for other women. It especially speaks to His sensitivity to moms-to-be.

The Scriptures tell us that a few days after being informed that her life will change forever, Mary headed to the hills of Judea to be with her cousin Elizabeth. The angel had mentioned her cousin to Mary as a reference point of God's miraculous power. Mary would now have a connection to another woman who was experiencing a miracle of her own.

News of Elizabeth's pregnancy had to be comforting to Mary. She may or may not have heard these wonderful, long-awaited tidings before the angel's visit. Information did not travel as quickly between towns in those days, especially when they were far apart. Nevertheless, Elizabeth's pregnancy became a gift to Mary in ways she could never have anticipated.

As Elizabeth's cousin, Mary had grown up knowing of

Elizabeth's infertility. In the culture in which they lived, a woman's value was greatly diminished if she was unable to bear her husband a child. Fortunately for Elizabeth, she had married a godly man, named Zechariah, whose love was not dependent on her womb.

There was probably a good fifty years' age difference between Mary and Elizabeth. Yet the moments they would share were far greater than the span of their lives. No doubt God knew Mary was going to need to be in the presence of another woman, someone whose wisdom and life experiences would point the way for her. By going to her cousin Elizabeth, she was able to give her family time to process her alarming news.

> God knew Mary was going to need to be in the presence of another woman, someone whose wisdom and life experiences would point the way for her.

We can only imagine what went through the minds of Mary's mom and dad. They probably needed time to digest the life-changing events for their family. News such as Mary's would cause shame for her entire clan, not just her immediate family. Mary's departure to be with a wise family member such as Elizabeth could only help the situation.

We also know that Joseph had to have his own encounter with the angel in order to accept Mary's divine pregnancy. It would be during Mary's time with Elizabeth that he would come to terms with the broader role he would play in the life of the Son of God.

God Allowed Mary Time to Adjust to Her New Role

Mary's arrival in Judea provided many blessings for both herself and Elizabeth. Think about this for a minute: A teenage cousin, pregnant with the Son of God, arrives at an old woman's house. Elizabeth is probably in her late sixties and is six months pregnant with John, the forerunner to Christ. Elizabeth must have known God was up to something special when she discovered the role her own child would play in the life of the Messiah. Thus, when Mary arrives at her door, all the pieces fall into place, and Elizabeth now understands her role in the Savior's story.

Mary's extended visit with Elizabeth allowed her the time she needed to be encouraged and mentored. It would give them time to talk about the things women need to talk about during pregnancy. It also allowed Elizabeth time to review the truths of Scripture that would be relevant to Mary as she moved forward with her new life. How awesome for the two of them to have each other!

The bond between them would also deepen because the miracle of their children's pending births would be something they would share for the rest of their lives. Mary needed to know that there would be at least one woman in her life who would grasp the intimacy a miracle would bring.

The three-month visit was also an indication of God's willingness to give Mary time to mature, get through the first trimester, and prepare for the challenges that would accompany her return to Nazareth. God is good to recognize the human condition of His people.

Being a female is a wonderful privilege. I have loved my ability to be a mother, carry a child in my womb, and nurse my baby. There were many years when I thought that would never be my reality. I remember the shock I experienced when Dr. Sekine told me I was pregnant. I was holding my adopted five-month-old at the time, and needless to say, you could have knocked me over with a feather. I had longed to hear those words all my life, but when they came, they were as shocking as they were exciting. It took several days to absorb the news (though the morning sickness soon helped reality kick in).

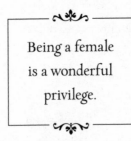

Being a female is a wonderful privilege.

The Gift Women Give Each Other

Women have lots of questions, fears, and concerns. Thoughtful, they want to know they're on the right path, making the right decisions, each becoming the right person through the process. The same holds true for moms too. No matter how old she happens to be, the unknown of the labor and delivery process adds stress to any first-time mom in waiting. Women gain great comfort from sharing with one another because women understand other women at a level that facilitates strength and hope.

Because I have worked with mothers for several decades, I have listened to hundreds of birthing stories. Each mom's story is chiseled in her memory bank, and regardless of her stage in life, she will never forget the details of her baby's birth. Like a soldier returning from battle, a woman has a "war story" too: her birthing experience.

In the Jewish culture, women spent a lot of time together. They walked to the well together to get water twice a day, and during this time they would socialize and chat. They helped deliver each other's babies and would tend to new moms during their first several months of motherhood. There was no problem too big for the circle of women to address or confront. They understood their role, trained up the younger women to assume it when the time arrived, and would remain a source of constant counsel and support throughout their lives.

> Like a soldier returning from battle, a woman has a "war story" too: her birthing experience.

Today's woman is no different from the first-century one. She has the same needs as those in Mary's time. Women of this generation, however, live more isolated lives and tend to tackle the challenges of motherhood, as well as life, on their own. In our current, transient world, women are fearful of making attachments to other women, being vulnerable with their struggles, and asking for help from others. They are also afraid of being judged, criticized, and rejected in the secret places of their lives. For moms, the most vulnerable place in their hearts tends to be their motherhood.

I recently met with a group of single moms attending a seminar designed to address their unique needs. On this particular day, we offered each mom the opportunity to be partnered with a mentor. As I read through their applications, I was saddened at the high number of the women who had difficult relationships with their mothers. More than 60 percent reported that they had either a poor, awful, or nonexistent relationship with their mothers. How profound that so many of these moms suffer from a lack of maternal support and encouragement.

As I continued reading the applications, I was further saddened by their statements about what they longed to hear from their moms: "I am really glad you are my daughter," "You are a good mother," and "How can I help you?" were just a few of the examples these mothers shared. In essence, they were simply looking for someone they valued and loved, who would, in turn, validate their own worth. What word of encouragement or acceptance have you longed to hear from your mom? Some of us take things like this for granted because it has been our normal to have women who care about us. If you look around in your circle of friends, however, you will see women in need of a listening ear, a caring heart, and a shoulder on which to lean.

> From the beginning of time, women have taught each other their place in society.

Families, communities, and the world will always be better when we encourage women to embrace their roles as mentors, teachers, and friends. From the beginning of time, women have taught each other their place in society. It has only been in the last hundred years that women have become so isolated from a support system.

Every woman's story is different and unique to her. Some

parts of her journey will be private and personal. We can take our cue from Mary, however, who knew that to reach out in her time of need would be the way God would meet her in her most vulnerable moment. Being a friend or mentor does not require magic answers, perfect children, or a great deal of time. It simply requires a desire to make a difference in a woman's life: listening, loving, and sharing hope.

EIGHT

MARY'S TRUE LEGACY–HER FAITH

MARY KNEW FAITH WOULD BE HER WITNESS

"Blessed is she who believed, for there will be a fulfillment of those things which were told her from the Lord."

—LUKE 1:45

Many women who have heard Mary's story—and many preachers who teach on Luke's account of Jesus' birth—reflect on the immense call to faith the angel Gabriel presented to Mary. She knew her response would set the course for her witness. And God in His graciousness knew her faith would require confirmation each step of the way. The first instance of this confirmation came from Elizabeth:

> At that time Mary got ready and hurried to a town in the hill country of Judea, where she entered Zechariah's home and greeted Elizabeth. When Elizabeth heard Mary's greeting, the baby leaped in her womb, and Elizabeth was filled with the Holy Spirit. In a loud voice she exclaimed: "Blessed are you among women, and blessed is the child you will bear! But why am I so favored, that the mother of my Lord should come to me? As soon as the sound of your greeting reached my ears, the baby in my womb leaped for joy." (Luke 1:39–44 NIV)

What a moment this must have been for Mary! Elizabeth's welcoming Mary was a supernatural encounter for both women and one that must have brought great comfort to the younger woman's heart.

Upon Mary's greeting to Elizabeth, the baby in Elizabeth's womb started doing jumping jacks. The Holy Spirit had come upon Elizabeth, and any time the presence of the Lord enters our lives, things happen. Elizabeth was a seasoned, mature believer and recognized how God worked. As a result, she knew to listen, trust, and welcome God's entry into the moment.

We can see that the truth that applied to Mary also applied to Elizabeth: God will allow His Spirit to come upon us. This verse confirms that what God was doing with Mary, He would also do for Elizabeth. They would not raise their sons alone and in their own wisdom. They would have access to heaven itself to raise their boys. The good news for today's moms is that they, too, can have that same assurance.

Elizabeth marveled that the mother of Christ had entered her home and was blessing her with her presence. I am sure this unexpected declaration surprised Mary. A youthful maiden being hailed as a blessing by an older, mature relative had to be a surreal moment in Mary's short life, but it would be a memory she would call on in moments when she felt alone and abandoned.

Elizabeth's comment that Mary is "favored among women" acknowledges the girl's once-in-a-lifetime role and its significance for all women for all of time. Elizabeth understood the import of God's selection of Mary. She was elated not only because she was related to Mary, but also because she could now walk alongside her through this profound moment.

The most amazing element of Elizabeth's declaration, however, is her acknowledgment of Mary's faith. She understood the remarkable step Mary had taken in trusting God with her life. She praised Mary for her confidence that what the angel had said would come to pass. Being spiritually mature, she knew that believing what Mary was being asked to believe would be no small task.

Mary's legacy begins to be defined in this moment. The angel tells her the role she will play in the Messiah's story, but Elizabeth tells her that her faith will be her greatest witness for all generations. This is evidenced by the existence of the book of Luke.

Legacy is another way to reflect on Mary's role in history. She was focused on being faithful to the God who knew her so well. She trusted that if she obeyed and walked the journey God had laid before her, she would be at peace, knowing she had pleased Him. While she did not know all that lay ahead, she knew He would be with her.

I am convinced Mary was not concerned about her place in history. Like any new expectant mom, her focus was

> All of us will leave an imprint on those we leave behind. The question is simply, what will it be?

on her pregnancy, her family, and becoming a good mom. While she had some understanding of her son's future, she stayed present in the moment to take each day as it came.

Examination of Mary's faith and how it impacted Elizabeth is an invitation for all women and mothers of every stage and age to reflect upon the impact they are having. All of us will leave an imprint on those we leave behind. The question is simply, what will it be?

What Shall I Give Them?

Today's culture has forced women to diligently focus on the here and now. What does my job require of me today? Should we move to another city to advance my husband's career? Is this house in the right school district? Should I go back to school? What talents do I need to develop in my children? Do they have what it takes to succeed? Questions like these are valuable and necessary, but they will fall short if everything they focus on is short-term or solely about children's immediate needs.

> Women need to be attentive to who *they* are and the faith *they* possess, and there is no exception for moms while they are raising their children.

Women need to be attentive to who *they* are and the faith *they* possess, and there is no exception for moms while they are raising their children. In years to come, the children will not remember what sacrifices their moms made to get them into the "right" school, but they will recall the strength of faith and character their moms possessed when tough times arrived.

When I was thirteen, my maternal grandmother, whom I called GiGi, was killed at age sixty by a drunk driver. GiGi was my biggest fan and my greatest hero. Her mom had died in childbirth when GiGi was two, and six months later, GiGi came down with polio. She overcame tremendous odds and challenges, ones that would have destroyed many. GiGi, however, chose to let these difficulties make her stronger and her faith deeper.

As the granddaughter of such an amazing woman, I learned so much from her in the short time she was in my life. She loved me unconditionally, and every teenage girl needs to feel that type of love. I had just spent the summer with GiGi, being encouraged, loved, and valued in a season when many teens that age feel awkward, alone, and fragile. I had only been home a few days when she was killed.

I felt raw pain that I cannot begin to describe. What was even worse was seeing my own mom suffer in a way I had never experienced. The most important woman in my life was now grieving the loss of the most important woman in hers. How would we cope? What would we do with the injustice of what had happened?

In the early days after my grandmother's death, we grieved and mourned. We could not hide or deny the pain, because it was just so deep. Yet, in the midst of that horrific time, my mother modeled for me a heart of faith and grace I knew had come only from God. "Cathy, I do not know why God allowed this to happen, and I am so sad Mother is gone, but in moments like these, I have to trust Him. We may never understand why this happened, but what I do believe is that God knows what He is doing," said my mom.

Even in my mother's deepest sorrow, she still chose to believe in the goodness of God. She would later tell me that she felt as though God had allowed the fatal accident in order to protect her mom from suffering she would have experienced as the result of heartaches in her own children's lives. Tragedy would strike my mom's family many times after GiGi's death, but she was spared the heartbreak of it all.

> Even in my mother's deepest sorrow, she still chose to believe in the goodness of God.

The second gift of faith my mother gave me in that sad season of our lives was her merciful attitude toward the drunk driver. She thought he should never be allowed to drive again, so no one else would suffer the same type of loss, but bitterness and resentment were not her focus. Instead, she chose to place her attention on being a woman who would most reflect the nature and character her mother had taught her. She wanted to be sure she reflected the faith that had been lived before her, and she knew it would not include pity, victimization, or revenge. The greatest honor my mom could bestow upon my grandmother's legacy was to carry on in the spirit of her faith.

I am not saying it is wrong to be angry over wrongful deaths or that a woman is weak in faith if she expresses sadness, frustration, and hurt. All of these emotions are appropriate when people we love have died prematurely. It is important, however, that we walk *through* the process of grief and not get stuck in our anger. I have known too many people who ceased to live after the death of someone they loved. For women who have faith, we will want to find our way back to a vibrant life so our legacy will be one such as Mary's.

The mother of Christ would have her faith tested throughout her journey. Today's moms need to recognize that their faith, too, will be tested. So many times when we face a difficult season or challenge, we do not think about the impact our fear, skepticism, and doubt can have on our families. But the truth is that mothers control the temperature of the home, and when we handle things with faith, our children will be stronger for it.

> Intentional moms recognize and appreciate the importance of having a kingdom focus.

Women need to become more mindful of who they are and how they impact their families. Any mom can focus on the here and now, but intentional moms recognize and appreciate the importance of having a kingdom focus. When our attention is directed on developing the heart, character, and faith of our children, we will take a different route to accomplish our goals. Our faith life can lay the foundation for how our children see, trust, and know God. Even if our children go through a season of rebelling or questioning the existence of God, we can be comforted and regret-free if we know we have authentically shown them a life that was based upon our faith in Christ.

Walking the Difficult Journey

Elizabeth's life experience, scriptural knowledge, and spiritual wisdom clearly reveal her understanding of Mary's future trials. When she blessed Mary for having the faith she possessed, she knew it was going to be paramount for the young mother to walk through the struggles that lay ahead. No woman could ever endure the righteous indignation of her son's abuse and death without a supernatural portion of faith to maintain hope in the midst of horror.

> To have faith in the midst of turmoil or the unknown is the true revelation of what we believe about the character and nature of God.

When things are well and life is good, it is easy to believe. The real test comes when life is falling apart and we have no idea what is going to happen next. To have faith in the midst of turmoil or the unknown is the true revelation of what we believe about the character and nature of God. Elizabeth's blessing of Mary's confidence in God was a gift to her because it reinforced what she would need as her journey unfolded. It also would be a memory for Mary to cherish in those difficult moments that would remind her of the Source of her strength.

What is the witness of your faith? May it be said of all of us: "Blessed is she who has believed . . ."

NINE

A BOLD DECLARATION

MARY KNEW TO HAVE A HEART OF PRAISE

*And Mary said, "My soul magnifies the Lord, and
my spirit rejoices in God my Savior . . ."*

—LUKE 1:46 ESV

U pon Elizabeth's pronouncement of blessing upon Mary, we see a marvelous and wondrous response from this Jewish maiden. We do not see a timid and frightened virgin but a bold and courageous young woman whose depth is revealed in a declaration of praise and thanksgiving. What a moment this must have been for Elizabeth!

Once again what boggles the mind is Mary's amazing awareness of all the variables that come into play at one time. Her discernment is phenomenal, and her ability to recognize humankind's major foibles at such an early age reflects another reason why God selected her for her role as mother. She not only understood her humble heritage, but she also recognized the sinful nature of humanity and the need for a Savior.

Most adolescent girls are rather self-absorbed. This is not a criticism or a put-down. Developmental psychologists have long understood that adolescence is a time of self-discovery and burgeoning independence. This season is not typically known for higher levels of thought, but instead for introspection of one's self and purpose. Mary was clearly mature and wise beyond her years. But how did she become this way?

Many would say that God bestowed special gifts of wisdom and discernment upon her. Nevertheless, she was still a girl from lowly beginnings who experienced life much like most females of her day. Her small village was her place of reference, where she observed firsthand the ways of man. Her knowledge of people as well as her ability to comprehend their need would prepare her for her role as the mother of the Savior.

Thus, her declaration of praise is the culmination of her knowledge of God's faithfulness to His people and a reflection of her faith voiced aloud for all the world to know and hear. It is the first time we get a full picture of her testifying of her lowly state amid the grand and glorious God she willingly and lovingly serves. In this moment, she wants everyone who can hear to know how wonderful God is and how faithful He is to care for the very children who have turned against Him. It is in this moment that we know she sees God's purpose and the reason she is carrying His Son.

Mary's Praise Reflects Her Knowledge of God

This passage from Luke reveals several important truths about Mary. We are exposed to a young woman who demonstrates her maturity on an intellectual and spiritual level. Her ability to identify example after example of God's relationship with His people is amazing. She recognizes Him for His patience, enduring love, and willingness to deal with the proud and arrogant.

Mary's knowledge reflected a studious heart, a woman who knew that history would be an indicator of the future. If she could look back and count on God to deal with the challenges and injustices of life in the past, she knew she could count on Him to be with her as her mysterious life unfolded. Never before would she need to be as confident in this truth as she would now.

As Mary raised Jesus, she was able to share her personal knowledge of God along with the rabbinic training He received. Her perspective was field-tested and life-worn, while the Jewish training was very historical and doctrinal. Her knowledge gave credibility to her praise and showed Jesus additional relevancy to the purpose of praise.

> Mary's knowledge reflected a studious heart, a woman who knew that history would be an indicator of the future.

In today's culture, moms are inundated with information on parenting. In fact, in 2011, there were more than twenty-nine thousand books a mom could purchase on how to be a good parent. When you add to this list websites, blogs, and numerous other resources, it is easy to see how mothers can become paralyzed when trying to decide what to read or where to turn for help.

If Mary were alive today, I have no doubt that she would not do things much differently with Jesus. She translated the scriptural knowledge she possessed into her daily existence, including her motherhood role. She also knew that praise was a reminder of God's intervention in the history of her people, so it was a comfort to focus on the source of her peace and hope.

The Praise Is for God Alone

It has often been said that praise is the only part of prayer that has nothing to do with the human condition and everything to do with the heart of God. Mary's monologue of praise reveals her heart of adoration for her God and her desire to acknowledge Him for who He is and what He is doing. Her praise is for Him and Him alone.

As a culture, we have become very self-absorbed. Although many of us desire to be other-centric, the reality is, we have a tendency to be the object of our universe. I think it is one of the reasons we often struggle with praise.

In this series of verses, Mary reveals many elements of her relationship with God. She acknowledges that He is the only one who could do what He has done. She totally grasps the enormity of God and showers Him with adoration for His sovereignty. She totally gets that He is in the details of her life while at the same time acknowledging that He is the true Alpha and Omega, the beginning and the end.

What comes out so powerfully in this series of verses is Mary's ability to articulate the breadth of God's intimacy with human life. This teenage girl makes reference to something more important than her knowledge of what God has done: she understands the nature of who God *is*. Clearly she has experienced revelation from Him that changed her life.

For most of us, praise is the area of our prayer life that gets the least attention and time. First of all, most of us are in a hurry, so we don't make time to offer something that we think God already knows. We barely get to the thank-yous for what He has done before we move on to asking Him for something or telling Him what we don't like about what is happening. Thus, praise slips through the cracks, and God doesn't get what is to be totally for Him.

> For most of us, praise is the area of our prayer life that gets the least attention and time.

It also seems that people in general are uncomfortable with praise, regardless of whom it is for or from. Most women I know struggle when they are praised because they don't know what to do with it. If they receive it, they are fearful that people may believe they are arrogant. When they don't receive it, it makes them look insecure. Thus, they stumble and as a result, fail to be a role model on how to receive a compliment well.

Praise has also received a bad rap because many people have used it in a false or hypocritical way. Recipients are often skeptical when they hear a compliment because they question the sincerity of its source or doubt its accuracy. Thus, skepticism in general has made praise a more complicated process. The last thing anyone wants to be is a hypocrite with God, so if they cannot sincerely adore Him, they don't even try.

Praise is honestly complimenting God for being who He is. When children hear moms compliment or praise God, they are providing them a wonderful opportunity to hear a pure heart demonstrate a healthy example of loving God well. Regardless of their age, children whose moms sincerely adore God in their hearing are forming a foundation of true worship.

Praise as a Way of Life

Mary's ability to so thoroughly focus on who God is and what He had done is a testimony of her selflessness and maturity. She never lost sight of the fact that her gift to God was a time of isolated focus upon Him. She wanted to bless Him for all that He is.

> It was important for Mary to have a heart of praise if she was to raise the Son of God.

It was important for Mary to have a heart of praise if she was to raise the Son of God. We see how naturally it flowed from her lips—it must have been a way of life for her. No doubt God wanted to give His Son an earthly example of the role praise was to play in the life of a believer; Mary reflected such a heart.

Habits are formed from repetition. For praise to be a way of life in our homes and lives, it has to become a healthy habit. Needless to say, we have to make it a priority.

Being an intentional mom means a mother will develop a laser focus on a belief, value, or priority. This mind-set applies to action as well as thought so that her conviction stays on the radar screen of her life. Let me give you an example.

When a family says a blessing at the table before they eat,

they are modeling for their children an attitude of gratitude. When this behavior is a habit, children will not eat until they have said a prayer and they will often not let others eat until the blessing has been given.

Praise was a normal part of life for Jesus because it was life breathing. He grew up knowing the power of praise, and it would never have dawned on Him to not demonstrate His adoration to His Father God. No doubt, Jesus was a reflection of His mother's heart. Throughout the Gospels, we see Jesus taking the time to be with His Father, praising Him and thanking Him for His presence and His faithfulness. Whether it was while performing a miracle, teaching the disciples, or being alone with God, Jesus knew the importance of praise.

Moms can learn a lot about who they are by observing their children. Children mimic our habits, nuances, and patterns whether we want them to or not. Thus, when we watch our children, they will unearth painful insights and questions:

- Do I have a heart of praise, or do I reflect a critical spirit?
- Have my children witnessed a mom who regularly praises her God?
- What do I want my praise legacy to be?

For women without children, what would your closest (most honest) friends say about you? Questions like these are not designed to create guilt. They are an invitation to stop and reflect on this ever-important opportunity to connect to our

Creator. By paying attention to this part of our faith life, we will strengthen our impact on our friends and family by modeling for them an example of humility and God-dependence in every situation.

TEN

EMBRACING THE UNKNOWN

MARY KNEW BEING A MOTHER WOULD TAKE HER TO DIFFICULT PLACES

Joseph also went up from Galilee, out of the city of Nazareth, into Judea, to the city of David, which is called Bethlehem, because he was of the house and lineage of David.

—LUKE 2:4

Mary's return home from her time with Elizabeth must have been an unsettling time for Mary. She was returning to a village that was skeptical of her pregnancy story. Her family had probably absorbed the judgment and hostility surrounding her news while she was gone, but they could protect her no more. It would now be Joseph's place to step in and defend his new wife.

During the months leading up to their departure to Bethlehem, they married, set up their home, and established a life together. Scripture tells us they did not engage in sex prior to the birth of Christ. Truth be told, sex was probably the last thing on their minds considering the assignment they had received and the challenges they were encountering.

A couple of months before Jesus' arrival, Caesar Augustus sent out a decree that the entire Roman Empire should be taxed. This decree would require that every man return to the city of his birth so a census could be taken and taxes paid. There was a time frame on this decree, and Mary's delivery date was in the middle of it.

Joseph knew he had to obey the law. He also knew he must keep Mary by his side. The situation for her and the baby was too dangerous to leave her behind, even though she would be with family. God had entrusted Joseph to be her husband and the earthly father to His Son. Joseph did not want to relinquish the responsibility to anyone else; he was to be the leader in his home.

Joseph knew the trip would be hard on Mary both physically and emotionally. Although he had never been through a pregnancy before, he had been around family and friends enough to know that the last months were particularly difficult. But Joseph also knew that Mary was spiritually strong and could overcome whatever they were to face.

Thus, their journey began.

Mary Knew Her Life Would Be Unpredictable

Mary's departure from Bethlehem was more than a simple good-bye to her family. She would say, "So long" to the safety and comfort of the familiar as well as release her definition of normal to God. This is no small task for a young woman who is about to birth the Son of God.

Many of us enjoy the adventure life can bring and appreciate the unexpected moments when they come into our lives. However, most pregnant moms want their pregnancies to be textbook. They want everything to fall into the category of "normal" so their babies will develop well and be healthy. Riding a donkey one hundred miles in 80- or 90-degree heat did not fall into that category.

One of my personal beliefs about the motherhood process is that it is really God's first lesson in teaching us that we are not in control. Few of us actually have a baby when we want, much less in the manner in which we want the process to go.

Some of us think we are going to get pregnant in a few months and it takes years. Some of us want to deliver our babies naturally, but end up having a C-section. Some of us think conception will be easy, yet find adoption to be the only answer.

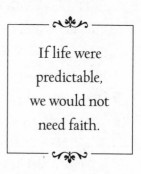

If life were predictable, we would not need faith.

Being the mother of adult children, I can honestly see how God wanted to break me from my own self-reliance to become God-dependent; He used my kids' births to begin that ever-so-important lesson. If only I had gotten the lesson more quickly!

If life were predictable, we would not need faith. We would unfold like an assembly line, and the predictable would happen. It would also leave us empty and dull, not living the life intended for a child of God.

Mary Knew Parenting a Savior Would Include Pain

When we become moms, we have a tendency to stay in the moment. We do not focus on the future or the possibilities of what can be because it can be frightening. In many ways, that is a healthy perspective to have, because the Bible warns us that worry should not have a place in our lives. Nonetheless, Mary recognized that there would be a cost to being the mother of Jesus, and she knew it would include pain.

Pain can come in many forms for a mother. Some pain involves physical challenges or difficulties that children and teens face. Not every child is blessed with coordination or the ability to do the simple things easily. Some struggle with a handicap that will be a part of their lives forever. Watching a child suffer from bodily pain tests every mom at the core of her being, regardless of the child's age. Mary wasn't clued in on what her son would eventually experience, but she knew the Scriptures well enough to know He would suffer.

Mary also knew that being the Son of God would create emotional pain for her son as well as for her own heart. There is nothing more painful for a mom than to observe her child being rejected. That has caused many a mother to do inappropriate things. When a mother's broken heart prohibits her from manifesting good judgment, it can create a crisis of immense proportions. Mary's future included moments that would drive even the healthiest of mothers to the brink of insanity. Fortunately for Jesus, as well as all believers to come, Mary turned her pain over to her God. As a result, she not only endured but also overcame the darkness her pain brought.

Mary Knew That No One Would Understand Her Son

I take great comfort in this part of Mary's story. When a mother is chosen to raise a child few others understand, it is a lonely and painful existence. If ever a mother had the perfect child, it was Mary. What was not perfect was the way other people perceived Him and the comments she must have over-heard about Him.

I can just imagine being at the well with the other moms. As Mary went to get her day's water for cooking, she was probably chided, questioned, and judged. Her son thought differently, obeyed easily, and possessed a gentle spirit. Until her later children were born, she had nothing to offer the conversation with other moms about how to discipline a stubborn child or deal with a sneaky boy. He was clearly different and every-one could see He did not fit the norm.

> When a mother is chosen to raise a child few others understand, it is a lonely and painful existence.

Rejection for being "good" is still rejection. It still hurts a mother's heart and makes her sad. We do not have an account of how Mary felt during the early years of her par-enting, but what we do know is that she would encounter the emotions any mother would.

One of the most painful parts of my role in ministering to women is listening to moms who are raising children who do not "fit in." This can take the form of rejection by their peers, or at times, even their own family. These moms are angry, hurting, and sad. They are frustrated that other people do not see what they see in their children and feel overwhelmed by the aloneness their sons or daughters experience.

I, too, raised a child no one understood. He was referred

to as "different" or "odd." Most people wrote his differences off to his intellect, much as they would an absentminded professor. I heard "friends," church members, and even family members make comments about him that broke my heart. Every mother is fiercely protective of her children and would do anything for them. So you can imagine my hurt, dismay, and anger over hearing such injustice toward my son. Though I never portrayed such emotions externally, the tears I wept and the pain I felt as his mom were at times overwhelming. Fortunately, I never resorted to violence, but tears from the pain easily flowed out of me.

How much more would Mary have felt the anguish of Jesus' journey? She knew the cause was worth it, but the price was costly. Not only would she feel His pain, but she would carry her own for the rest of her life. This type of loneliness was something she had probably not heard other moms discuss. Even today, few moms will admit to the pain they experience. Many are fearful that if they are honest about it, it will somehow reflect poorly on their children. The reality is that when a mom can be honest with other moms, she will often find comfort, support, and encouragement.

> Mary's loneliness in raising Jesus would actually be a gift to her because it would force her back into the arms of her God.

Never would there be a life more scrutinized than the one Jesus would live. Mary's loneliness in raising Jesus would actually be a gift to her because it would force her back into the arms of her God. It would give her an opportunity to pour out her heart to Him and experience His comfort in the midst of her pain.

Another gift of her motherhood loneliness is that she would be able to model for Jesus the way to handle loneliness in a manner that would bring honor to God and strength to their faith. Mary clearly understood that her life was an example for Jesus in many ways, and she never lost track of the importance of living a life of integrity.

As I have reflected on the great thinkers and theologians of our time, most of them have experienced deep levels of isolation. Some of them sought their solitude, while others experienced it because it was forced upon them. Regardless of the source, the sense of being all alone produced a deepening of the soul as well as a meaningful dependency on God.

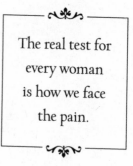

The real test for every woman is how we face the pain.

Womanhood and motherhood will take us to difficult places throughout the course of our lives. The question is not *if* these times will come, but *when*. The real test for every woman is how we face the pain and what example we give those around us when facing the difficult moments. I always told my kids when they were growing up that I would learn more about who they were in times of disappointment and difficulty than during victory and success. The same can be said about us as moms. Let's make sure we do not waste these challenges to know God in our most vulnerable moments.

ELEVEN

A REFLECTIVE HEART

MARY KNEW SHE NEEDED TO PONDER

*But Mary kept all these things and pondered them
in her heart.*

—LUKE 2:19

Taylor had been born, and we had received word that all had gone well. My personal physician had delivered him, so I knew there would be extra interest and care given to both the birth mom and our new son. Dr. Sekine called to deliver the news, and I could sense that he was as excited as we were.

We had told our attorney we did not want to see or hold Taylor until the papers had been signed by both parents. Neil and I knew we could not cope with the possibility of getting attached to this little boy, only to have to give him back. We would only have to wait thirty-six hours before the legalities were completed, but they seemed like thirty-six years.

We got the call telling us to come to the third floor of the hospital. This was the first time that hospital had ever allowed adoptive couples to be a part of the child's life before the moment of discharge. Thus, it was a new experience for all of us.

Neil and I were ushered into a makeshift room that had previously been used as a storage area. It was equipped with a rocking chair, a baby bed, and a couple of other chairs. We were not allowed to have visitors because of the confidentiality element for both the birth mom and the child. We waited anxiously for Dr. Sekine to bring us our new son.

About thirty minutes after our arrival, Dr. Sekine walked in and came toward me. "Mrs. Hickem, I am proud to present to you your little boy!" With that, he placed Taylor in my arms.

Neil and I just stood in awe, looking into his eyes and telling him who we were and who he was. For Neil and me, it was a moment frozen in time. Our long, frustrating journey had come to an end with a miracle we had never anticipated. In that moment, all the sadness, pain, and emptiness of the previous years dissipated, and joy set in.

Dr. Sekine, Neil, and I spent the next several hours with our new son. Dr. Sekine had become a dear friend through our infertility journey and his presence was both a comfort and a gift. When the doctor left the room, Neil went to get us some lunch from the hospital cafeteria.

Like most moms when left alone with their child for the first time, I felt so many thoughts and feelings flood in at a rampant pace. I unwrapped Taylor from his blanket and looked at his little fingers and toes. Taylor stared back without much of a whimper. It appeared that he was checking me out as much as I was studying him.

In the moments that followed, I heard a voice in my head, the one I had learned was God speaking to me. It was not an audible voice, but one where thoughts came that I knew were not my own.

"Cathy, Taylor is the second son I have given you. The first one's name is Jesus."

All of time stopped in that moment, and I wept. I realized that just as God had given up His Son, Jesus, for me, God had just given me this little boy. He gave us Taylor simply because He loved us, no more and no less. It was in the stillness that I could reflect on our journey and see that God had been with us all along. My story portrays a small glimpse of what Mary experienced. No doubt, you have a similar story of your journey and a moment of awe.

Time must have stopped for Mary on the evening of Jesus' birth. The skies opened with angelic voices singing praises and giving glory to God for what He had done. What an amazing time it must have been for this new mother. The physical discomfort that accompanies delivery probably evaporated from her awareness as she stopped to drink in all that the moment held. Mary had not only given birth to a child, but she had been a part of God's promises being fulfilled.

Mary's Memories Would Sustain Her

From all accounts in Scripture, it appears as if Mary was the only female present when Jesus was born. It was extremely unusual for a Jewish woman to give birth alone, but this was to be a part of her story. Add to it the awkwardness that might have existed between Joseph and Mary since they had never experienced physical intimacy as a couple. Between the pain of childbirth, the strange surroundings of the birthplace, and the majestic welcome, Mary was saturated with a perspective that captured all of her senses.

I could imagine that Mary, like most women, noticed the details that surrounded that night. She appreciated Joseph's gentleness and attentiveness. She knew that this experience had challenged him in many ways, but she also knew she was safe because God was with him.

The smell of the hay, the sound of her baby sucking for the first time, and the excitement in the shepherds' voices may have been part of her birthing experience. Swaddling her baby and placing Him in a manger would be details she would share when she told her birth story to her family and friends. But there would be moments she would not share because they were meant just for her. It would be these intimate thoughts that would remind her of the bigger story of Jesus' birth.

To *ponder* as Mary did, women must take time to think deeply through their lives and the lives of their families.

God would use Mary's memories of Jesus' divine birth to sustain her faith when the dark moments of her motherhood journey would arise. By allowing Mary to see how intimately He was involved in the details of Jesus' birth, it would give her comfort to know He was equally concerned about the rest of His life.

Mary was a reflective woman, and this is one of the reasons she was chosen to be the mother of Christ. God needed her to be a woman who would pay attention to His direction and learn from the experiences she would encounter. Her ability to process all that was happening would be one of the ways God would impart wisdom to her as she parented Jesus.

To *ponder* as Mary did, women must take time to think deeply through their lives and the lives of their families. Most important, women must also think about the things and ways of God, meditating on who He is and how He is working in her life and family. This focus guides our decisions and allows us to be confident in all things because it is in the midst of those private places that she knows and hears the voice of God.

> Many of today's women are so busy "doing" life and motherhood that they overlook the deep themes of God's movement.

Many of today's women are so busy "doing" life and motherhood that they overlook the deep themes of God's movement. So many women have forgotten to *ponder* as Mary did. I have found that the women and mothers who take the time to reflect are better listeners, ask great questions, and possess the insight to know which dimension of themselves is needed in any situation. Reflective mothers pay attention to all the moving parts of each child's life, and that significantly increases the likelihood that they will truly know their children.

Over the last three decades, I have worked with families in a therapeutic environment. I have also been actively involved in the body of Christ, working with families of faith, who have embraced biblical truths as the foundation of their homes. In many of these families, there were several common denominators when it came to trouble and crises. One of these was a hurried mom who did not pay attention to her intuition.

Moms who take the time to ponder will be more likely to trust their God-given intuition. They will have thought through their children's personality types, strengths, weaknesses, friends, tendencies, etc. By truly knowing who her child is, an intentional mom will know when all is not well or when significant challenges have come their way.

God does not expect women to disappear into long stretches of solitude in order to be effective. What He does want for them is to be deliberate in making time to be still, to reflect, and to think about their children, their families, their God, and themselves. It is in these times that mothers will reap a harvest of peace, awareness, and direction in how to be the moms their families need.

Mary's Reflections Helped Her Prioritize

One of Mary's most significant attributes is her commitment to never losing sight of her responsibility to be the mother Jesus needed. This was critical for Jesus as an adult, even though many mothers today think their job is completed once the young adult leaves home. Mary allowed her relationship with God and Christ to be at the forefront of her priorities even amid the painful places she encountered both before and after her son left home.

Over the years, I have had the privilege of speaking with thousands of moms. From the pregnant mom-to-be to the ninety-plus-year-old mom who is worried about her family, I have heard many heart-wrenching stories of regret, sadness, and loss. In many of these stories, I would hear how things had slipped through the cracks. At first it didn't seem like a big deal. As time went by and the issues continued to grow, however, it was easy to go back and pinpoint when things fell apart. It would be when the mother lost sight of what really mattered by being distracted and failing to catch the signals her children, teens, and adult children were sending her. It was never her plan for this to happen, but because life managed her instead of her managing her life, she lost ground in her confidence as well as her relationships.

> How would you be different if your mom had taken the time to stay internally calibrated within and with God?

The world would look very different if women in it embraced a "ponder movement." How would you be different if your mom had taken the time to stay internally calibrated within and with God? Thinking deeply and acting intentionally can be a habit and way of life. Mary was just beginning her motherhood journey, but her habit of reflective thinking long before she was a mother would allow her to end it regret-free because she never lost sight of the importance of being a woman who pondered. Women in general and mothers would be happier and families would be healthier if we decided we wanted to reclaim this wonderful attribute Mary modeled for all.

TWELVE

THE GIFT OF OBEDIENCE

MARY KNEW OBEYING GOD WOULD HAVE ITS REWARDS

*And behold, there was a man in Jerusalem whose
name was Simeon, and this man was just and
devout, waiting for the Consolation of Israel, and
the Holy Spirit was upon him.*

—LUKE 2:25

Forty days after the birth of Christ, Mary and Joseph headed to the temple for her to offer a purification offering. This was customary for a woman since the blood associated with delivery made her ceremonially unclean. Being the faithful Jewish couple that they were, Joseph and Mary followed the Hebrew laws explicitly. They were, after all, raising a Jewish son who would be raised in the knowledge of the Pentateuch.

Unknown to both parents, God had led a "just and devout" man to the temple as they arrived. His name was Simeon, and God had promised him that he would not die before seeing the Messiah. What an amazing promise!

Upon seeing the infant, Simeon took Jesus into his arms and offered a blessing to God. He knew the promises that were held in this child and declared his gratitude for the fruition of this promise.

This is the only time in Scripture that we see Simeon's name appear. He gave a prayer of thanksgiving to God for the child

HEAVEN IN HER ARMS

Jesus, then turned and blessed Mary and Joseph. He acknowledged to them how God intended to use their son to redeem Israel
and told Mary that she would experience a broken heart as a part
of the redemption promise. Mary and Joseph were amazed at his
foreknowledge of what was to come.

As Simeon concluded his blessing upon the family, a widow
named Anna approached Simeon, Mary, Joseph, and the baby
Jesus. She, too, immediately broke out in praise and thanksgiving
for the role Jesus would play in the redemption of humankind.
This woman had lived in the temple for eighty-four years, praising and worshipping God. Her spirit was sensitive to the things
of God, so she intuitively knew when she walked toward Simeon
that the Christ child was there.

This passage of Scripture is not part of the nativity story,
but it is important when we are examining the lessons Mary's
life and obedience offer us. In this Hebrew ritual, we see a mom
who remembers the important tenets of her faith and acts in
obedience to her understanding of those beliefs. Being a new
mother, whose faith has brought her to this place, Mary's sacrifice in the temple was another way for her to demonstrate her
willingness to follow the law set forth in her Jewish faith.

Her encounters with Simeon and Anna were the unexpected
benefits of her obedience. God allowed her and Joseph to meet
two older people who had lived with the expectancy of God
delivering a Messiah to His people, and who boldly shared aloud
what God had done. I can just imagine the awe this young couple
must have felt in that moment!

How does this event in Mary's life apply to us? To begin

with, it gives us an example of the importance of a woman need-ing a personal journey in her relationship to her God. Mary recognized that it was not enough for her to be Jewish by heri-tage. If she was to raise the Son of God, she would need to have the integrity to practice what she preached.

In the midst of Mary's obedience to her faith, God showed up in an unexpected way and poured out blessings upon her and her family. This once again reminds us that blessings do not always come in the way we hope or expect them to, and it is never more obvious than in our parenting.

One of the main challenges I see today's woman facing, especially when she is trying to instill obedience in her children, is the issue of obedience without faith. Too many people give themselves over to religious rituals or practices, but their hearts are not in it. They go to church, but they do not believe the message. If faith isn't creating a notable difference in a woman's life and in parents' lives, it will probably not have the lasting impression internally. For moms, they are not setting up their own children for the lifelong journey of becoming like Christ—instead they are laying down a set of rules, not transformations of the heart.

There is no clearer example of children learning what they live than in the area of faith. In fact, one of the big hurdles I have seen people have to overcome is the hypocrisy they've witnessed in their parents. The double talk that can go on in our homes tells our children that our faith is just another thing for us to "do." Children—and teens especially—are not interested in living with Jekyll-and-Hyde parents, but ones who are consistent in growing,

> Authentic faith is powerful and, as Mary shows us, is the glue that keeps families together when tough times come.

learning, and becoming godlier people.

People do not expect perfection. What they want is a real faith manifesting itself in a real person who recognizes that they need God to help them with their daily lives. Authentic faith is powerful and, as Mary shows us, is the glue that keeps families together when tough times come. More important, it gives the children a model for the blessings that come from obeying the Lord.

The Reward of a Support System for Your Family

Simeon and Anna would be on the scene long enough to affirm Mary and Joseph in the initial stages of their parenting journey. They also symbolize another very important lesson we can learn about being a great mother: that we need other people to serve as role models and to speak blessings into our children's lives.

A healthy support system, as we've seen already, is important for the mother as well as the children. Never before have we seen such opportunities for moms to get together in small groups, clubs, and classes. Mothers are hungry to be their best, and fortunately, we are gaining momentum in this area of support.

Mothers will have to make a support system a priority, however, if they want to have a deeper well from which to draw. Having other women who have been through the journey ahead of me has been a source of wisdom that was free, encouraging, and filled with humor. It has also challenged me to think at a deeper level as well as learn from their mistakes. One of the first steps for mothers to be able to receive support is to admit that they actually need it.

As a mother, I wasn't looking to be perfect, nor did I expect to have perfect kids. What I did want was to know that I had done all I could in whatever situation we encountered. Having a support system gave me a wall to bounce against when I was at the end of my rope and allowed me to enjoy the successes with those who would appreciate what they meant to me as a mother.

Just as Simeon and Anna spoke blessings over Mary and Joseph's son, we need other people to encourage our children, and at times, to see things we do not yet see. Too many times I see mothers trying to be everything their children need. I especially see this with single moms who feel as if they have to play the part of both parents. Personally speaking, I do not think it can be accomplished; parenting is too big for one person, and it was never God's intention for us to do alone. Whether you are a single mom or a married mom who is simply trying to parent on your own, it was never God's intention for you to do this alone. Regardless of the environment in which you are parenting, God wants you to reach out to find the support that will help you create a network of people who love you and your family.

> One of the exciting ways God shows up is by bringing people into our lives who have strengths in our areas of weakness.

First of all, if we think we can do it all, we will give our children a very small world. One of the exciting ways God shows up is by bringing people into our lives who have strengths in our areas of weakness.

When Taylor was seventeen, he wanted to learn to cook. He mentioned it to me the summer before his senior year, so I realized I didn't have much time to teach him. Knowing that he was not interested in simple cooking techniques, but wanted an in-depth learning experience, I decided I needed some help.

I called eight sets of friends and asked them if they each would adopt Taylor for one Thursday during the summer and teach him how to prepare their favorite family meal. This would include him helping them purchase the ingredients, aiding in dinner preparation, dining with them, helping clean up, and coming home with the recipes in hand. Every friend I called graciously agreed to host Taylor that summer, and it was a wonderful experience on all fronts. Might I also add, he has become a wonderful cook!

With my daughter, I felt I needed to surround her with women who would speak into her life on a variety of levels. Some of the women had gifts I did not enjoy or possess. Other women had different personalities from mine, and their influence would give her a different perspective of life and living. These women represented a broad range of ages, backgrounds, and levels of spiritual maturity. All of them loved my daughter and spent time with her throughout her life.

When Tiffany graduated from high school, I had a quilt made using a square from each one of these women. We presented it to her at a lunch I put together in her honor that these women attended. I wanted her to take the quilt with her to school so that when she felt alone, doubted herself or God, and needed a hug, she could wrap herself in this quilt because it would represent all the loving arms that had hugged her through the years. This quilt was to symbolize their confidence in who she was and who God had created her to be.

I am so grateful for the men and women who loved my children and came alongside them the way they did. God used them to help my children grow in their thinking, their relationships, and their faith. They accepted my children for who they were and would stand in my place if for some reason Neil and I were absent. They loved them enough to be honest with them, but always loved them unconditionally. There really are no words to describe my heartfelt appreciation.

Likewise, Mary and Joseph were responsible for creating a support system for Jesus. They returned to their village when Jesus was two, and for the next twenty-eight years, He would be impacted by their friends and family. While we do not know any specific details of His relationships with them, what we do see is the evidence of a man who had healthy relationships, honored and respected women, and appreciated the value of a strong work ethic. These virtues, as well as many more, were instilled because Mary and Joseph lived obedient lives of faith and understood their greatest impact in Jesus' life would be lives lived with integrity, faith, and obedience.

WHEN ALL YOU CAN GIVE IS YOURSELF

MARY KNEW TO BE THERE WHEN THİNGS GOT TOUGH

"(Yes, a sword will pierce through your own soul also), that the thoughts of many hearts will be revealed."

—LUKE 2:35

Over the years, I have known new mothers who have received startling news within a few days of their babies' births. In most cases, it involved dangerous health issues with the baby. These mothers discovered that their newborn babies would have a lifelong battle with a disease, disorder, or disability. With their world quickly turned upside down, they would begin the lifelong journey of intervention, and sometimes, an all-out fight for survival.

Occasionally I would meet a mother who had serious complications from childbirth, and the residual effects of her delivery would be permanent. No mother goes into the delivery room thinking her new baby or her life will have dire consequences afterward. The mother will have to adjust to the news she receives because in the midst of fearing loss or death, she will need to focus on life and living.

Mary was placed in a similar situation when she heard the blessing Simeon pronounced upon her. In one verse, Simeon tells Mary that a sword will pierce through her soul also. His prophecy declared that the death of Christ would divide good from evil, but that Mary would also experience His crucifixion. The truth of this prophecy is further validated because Simeon speaks it to Mary alone, even though Joseph was with her. (Joseph died before the launch of Jesus' earthly ministry.)

Through the eyes of history, we can appreciate the depth of what this verse meant for all mothers. There is no greater pain for a mother than to witness her child suffering. Simeon captured this connection when he described how Mary's heart, too, would feel as if it were crucified. Can you imagine being told that your child would die and that it would feel as if it had happened to you?

This scripture, which has had little attention brought to it over the years, speaks volumes about how we define what constitutes a blessing. It also begs us to examine the intertwining of hearts and spirits when it comes to a mother and child.

> Mary also understood that not all things that come from God are easy.

Most of us assume that a blessing has a positive outcome. We like to think that when we ask God to bless our children, it will mean good things will happen to them or on their behalf. Yet, in the midst of this blessing from Simeon, difficult news was delivered to Mary. Obviously she would not rejoice at the thought of her newborn son dying a cruel death. News of his future would grieve her heart because this was her flesh and blood too.

Mary's awareness of her son's future death would make her heart heavy. This does not mean she was disobedient to God's plan for Jesus' life. What it signifies is that Mary had the heart of a mother who wanted her son to live and thrive. She understood that His journey was in the hands of the God whom she trusted. She also understood that not all things that come from God are easy.

In my own journey with God, I have discovered that God's *no*s in my life have often been challenging for me to grasp and comprehend. I wish I could tell you that I have had the maturity to always trust when things were hard and life was tough, but that would be a lie. Sometimes I have struggled with God, especially when it has come to my children. When injustice, suffering, or questions would arise that I could not fix and God would not remove, I would feel a mixture of emotions. Fortunately, I would eventually end up at the same place: *Do I trust in the sovereignty of God? Either I believe He is who He says He is, or I don't.* The answer to that question always helped me arrive at the best possible place.

> Do I trust in the sovereignty of God? Either I believe He is who He says He is, or I don't.

Being a mother was one of the best ways for God to relate to people. A parent-child relationship is the arena God uses to reveal some of His greatest truths in Scripture. God clearly understands the intimacy of a mother-child bond and equates it to the ultimate earthly bond. Maybe that is why the adage "A child is a mother's heart walking around outside her body" so resonates with mothers everywhere.

Motherhood Has a Cost

A woman who has been a mom for any length of time knows there is a cost to being a mother. The cost is beyond money or time. It involves her heart and soul, a part of her that can never be closed once it is open. She may also come to a place where she may be asked to die to her dreams or expectations for her child in order for God's ultimate plan to be implemented in both of their lives.

For all mothers, there will be times of joy and wonder as well as times of frustration and discouragement. Some moms will struggle with feeling worthy of their children, while others will question if God made a mistake with the children they received. Our role, which has been with us since the beginning of time, will push us to our limits in every capacity, with no guarantees that we will receive anything back as a reward for our sacrifice. All we can count on is the reality that we were chosen to mother our particular children and that God has a purpose for the ones we were entrusted to raise.

The pain of a mother's broken heart cannot be measured in human terms, for it reflects the mystery of God's heart in human terms.

The pain of a mother's broken heart cannot be measured in human terms, for it reflects the mystery of God's heart in human terms. For us to most reflect His character and nature, our ability to release our own suffering into His hands is a necessary part of our loving our children well. Let me explain.

Many a mother has spent five nights a week sitting at the dining room table, helping her learning-disabled child do his homework. What would take the average child a half hour to forty-five minutes to complete can drag out to three or more hours for a child with a learning disability. In the midst of this often frustrating experience, such a mother still has to care for the other children, cook dinner, give baths, help with the other needs of the home, and prepare her kids for bedtime. By the time her day is done, she collapses into bed, numb and weary, knowing the day will repeat itself with the rising of the sun.

Why would a mother tirelessly invest in her child day in and day out? Because she knows it is her responsibility to diligently believe in her child, and her steadfast spirit will be an example of godly love for her children. For all practical purposes, her job is thankless, but her calling to do it well was the voice to which she answered.

Mary Recognized That Her Presence Meant Something

In recent years, I have had the privilege of working with home-less mothers who were living in shelters. I have been blessed as well as encouraged when I met with them because in spite of their circumstances, they had a heart to make sure they loved their kids the best way possible.

Research has identified stressful home environments to be obstacles to healthy child development. My background as a psychotherapist had caused me to also expect high anxiety rates as well as disciplinary problems. This, however, was not always the case.

One strange observation I have made is that some homeless children have more access to their parents than the average kid. I found it fascinating that due to their circumstances, homeless mothers seemed to have an awareness of their children's individual personalities and interests that I would fail to see in some of society's more affluent families. As I began to study this phenomenon more closely, I discovered that many of the homeless children were well behaved and very loving, not at all what I had anticipated.

What I realized from my time with these homeless mothers and their children was that while the moms may not have

Nothing can replace a mother's presence in the life of her child.

much to give their kids in the way of the advantages our culture would deem helpful (extracurricular activities, tutoring, athletics, etc.), what they did have was their presence. Their look, their touch, their voices, and their attention communicated a value and comfort to their children that allowed their children's anxiety to decrease while their confidence increased. I recognize that this is not a scientific study but are simply observations that are worthy of further examination. Nonetheless, they register an important value: nothing can replace a mother's presence in the life of her child.

Mary would find herself with circumstances beyond her control. Yet what she could offer her son was her presence. She knew that as He grew, her role would change and her place would take a backseat to His earthly mission. Mary never lost sight of the knowledge that her greatest gift to her son would be the comfort of her presence and her faithfulness to be there when it counted most.

Godly Moms Love Best When Life Is at Its Worst

Another key lesson from Mary in Luke 2:35 is that good mothers love best when life is at its worst. She knew there would come a time when darkness would set into her soul because of the brutal battle her son would encounter. Yet she knew she would be there, no matter what. She had been present when the angels lit heaven with their rejoicing, and she would be there when the world went dark because of its sin. Under no circumstances would she let her son die alone!

No mother wants to watch her child die. It is the worst form of human pain known to humankind. Yet there is nothing more tragic than for a child to know that the very one who brought him into the world will not be there when he leaves it. Motherhood invites us to share in its greatest glories *and* its lowest moments. Mary teaches us that regardless of what we will face, we must do it with faith, dependency on God, and a commitment to enduring love.

FOURTEEN

EVERY WOMAN'S CHALLENGE IS LETTING GO

MARY KNEW SHE WOULD HAVE TO LET HER SON FULFILL HIS PURPOSE

[Jesus'] parents went to Jerusalem every year at the Feast of the Passover. And when He was twelve years old, they went up to Jerusalem according to the custom of the feast.

—LUKE 2:41–42

145

The story of twelve-year-old Jesus going to the Feast of the Passover is the only one that lets us experience the time between His birth and the launching of His earthly ministry. It is an extraordinary view into Jesus' relationship to Mary and one in which every mother can take comfort.

The family is off to Jerusalem for this annual feast, and Jesus travels with family and friends for this celebration. It is a significant event in the life of the Jewish family because it is a reminder of the bondage the Israelites endured for two hundred years. By celebrating their deliverance into freedom, they received a renewed awareness of their need for God.

The trip to Jerusalem would take many days. This religious ritual allowed friends and family to reunite for the celebration and enjoy a concentrated time of worship and Scripture study. They would sit at the feet of the rabbinical scholars and deepen their awareness of foundational truths of the Jewish law.

After the Passover Feast, Mary and Joseph begin the journey back with their family and friends. Chances are good that they can see the young teens and children from the village ahead of them, walking in the direction of Nazareth. They do not think anything of Jesus' whereabouts because they have always been able to count on Him to do what was expected. No doubt, this was a side of parenting Jesus that other mothers envied.

At some point in the journey homeward, Mary and Joseph begin to look for Jesus, only to realize He is nowhere to be found. They search everywhere among His friends and the crowd with whom they are traveling, only to come up empty-handed. Upon recognizing He is not with them, Mary and Joseph return to Jerusalem, panicked and frightened, hoping He is still there.

For three days, they have no idea where Jesus is. Can you imagine? I remember once losing sight of Taylor in a department store for about thirty seconds, and I was totally panic-stricken. The fear that set in was so overwhelming, I could barely breathe. To lose a child for three days would have made me lose my mind.

Fortunately for Jesus, Mary and Joseph manage to keep their emotions in check so they can proceed with their search. Upon arriving in Jerusalem, they head in the direction of where the rabbis were teaching and discussing the Scriptures, only to see their son sitting among the most learned Hebrew scholars. They watch as Jesus answers deep theological questions with comfort and ease, astonishing the teachers gathered around him. All who heard Jesus were amazed at His understanding and marveled at the depth of the questions He placed before them.

Mary's observance of Jesus' place amid the scholars must have been deeply moving. On one hand, the prophecies of the past of who He was and whose He was came alive in a new and fresh way. As Mary listened to Jesus' mature responses, she had to be internally proud and grateful that she was witnessing the fruition of God's promises.

This moment in the relationship between Mary and Jesus, however, takes on a new meaning. It is the first time we see Mary question Jesus' behavior. She asks, "Why have You done this to us? Look, Your father and I have sought You anxiously" (Luke 2:48). Mary is upset that Jesus stayed behind without considering them or communicating His plan. In fact, she has taken His actions personally, as if He has done this to them intentionally. She is obviously struggling with the whole experience.

The Tension of the Moment

So how do we handle this moment? Clearly, the young Messiah is being chastised by His mother, but He is the Son of God and incapable of sin. Mary is filled with righteous frustration and fear, weary from being overwrought with panic. What are we to make of this tension between them?

In this moment, both are right. Jesus' response to Mary reveals His understanding of His higher call from His heavenly Father. "Why did you seek Me? Did you not know that I must be about My Father's business?" (v. 49) reveals the laser vision Jesus possessed for His life's purpose. He is clearly focused on maximizing His opportunity to know His Father better, and being in the temple is comfortable for Him because He is dwelling in His Father's residence.

Mary, too, has a laser purpose, and that is to make sure she stays intentional in raising the Son of God. The idea that she had *lost* Jesus has heightened her sense of responsibility, and she needs to address her concerns with Him. We see that even when Jesus takes the time to explain His priorities, Mary still does not comprehend what He means. Although Mary knows who Jesus is in the process of fulfilling God's plan, she cannot separate her role as His mother to interpret His divine position.

I love this part of the Mary story because we see a side of her that makes her real and touchable. Every mother can relate to the fear that accompanies losing a child. We can understand the overwhelming gratitude Mary experiences when she sees her son fulfilling God's promises. And we can connect with the heart of Mary in the moment when we question how our children think. The attitude and behaviors we see in Mary remind mothers everywhere that being a conscientious, questioning mother is indeed okay with God.

> Mary's example reminds us that being a good mother does not mean we will always understand our children.

Mary's example in this story further reminds us that being a good mother does not mean we will always understand our children. Mothers will face periods from their kids' infancy to their adulthood when they have more questions than answers, recognizing that the only constant in mothering the child is *change*. Times like these can be unsettling for a mother because of her overwhelming sense of responsibility and protection.

Another great lesson this story unveils surrounds the importance of mothers seeing their children and teens for who they are becoming. Mary was faced with a son whose identity was unfolding into that of a young man. While she viewed Him as her son, Jesus saw Himself as a young man acting responsibly. The difference in perceptions between two people who know each other well is extremely common, but can lead to great strain if not understood by both people.

The Realities of Relationships

Mothers often struggle with treating their young adult children with respect, understanding, and patience. Too often parents are tired of their parenting responsibility by the time the teen has completed high school. Instead of recognizing that this new adult season is filled with confusion, self-doubt, and anxiety, parents react to the impulsivity of the age and the roller-coaster of decision-making.

Mothers who have the best relationship with both their adolescents and their young adult children are those who change their approach and expectations as their children change. It is very important for mothers to adapt to the ever-changing emotional and developmental needs of their children. This sensitivity to their unfolding stages will communicate to the children that their parents are paying attention to who they are becoming.

A changing and maturing mother will be better equipped to position herself as a resource and guide, a dimension of motherhood that will naturally follow in relationships where the mother has exhibited healthy and respectful behavior toward her adult children. When moms continue to parent their adult children the way they parented when they were younger, they will miss out on an opportunity to move to the next level of an enriching parenting experience.

I recently spoke with a woman whom I will call Barb. She had three children who were grown and had families of their own. As she was sharing her motherhood history with me, she told me she could not be more surprised at how her children landed in life. The firstborn son, whom everyone thought was the star of the family, struggled in college and ended up dropping out after the second year. The middle child, who had struggled during her high school years, had a wonderful college experience and is enjoying a terrific career in the fashion industry. The baby of the family, the one everyone thought was spoiled, turned out to be a warm and sensitive young man who keeps an eye on his parents. Barb, clearly confused by her children's outcomes, reflected on their journey.

"I had so many expectations for my firstborn son, and they didn't pan out. Looking back on his life, there were signs that he was struggling, but I paid more attention to the things he did well instead of the areas I assumed he would overcome if he simply put his mind to it," Barb said.

"With my daughter, she struggled with learning disabilities, so I was just grateful she made it out of high school. I am elated at her success now, but I would be lying if I told you I knew she would do so well. I didn't give her sense of style, knack for design, and artistic flare the credit they deserved because I only measured success by a grade point average," she went on to say with a sigh.

"My last child succeeded in spite of us. To be honest, we were tired by the time he came along, so we did not spend the energy we should have to make him behave. We overindulged him, and he had to learn some lessons the hard way because we were lazy. Fortunately, he turned out well in spite of us," Barb said. "I feel like I was a good mother until they hit the high school years, and then I seemed to quit paying attention to all the signs they were sending me that told me who they were."

She is grateful she has a good relationship with all three children now, but admits she could have avoided some problems if she had been more adaptable and aware.

Mary faced what every mother faces as her children move from one stage to the next in life: the unknown. She would not be exempt from the challenges simply because she was raising the perfect child. The end of this story tells us that this season in Jesus' life would be enhanced because of her practice of pondering or thinking deeply about her relationship with Him. The continued practice of this habit was an indication that it had served her well throughout the earlier years of her motherhood. It also validated the importance she placed on listening, learning, and growing as a mother. Most

> Mary knew she would have to begin letting go so that her son could go on to fulfill His God-given purpose.

significantly, she knew that by taking the time to ponder and reflect, she would hear the voice of God more clearly.

Mary knew there was a time when she would have to begin letting go so that her son could go on to fulfill His God-given purpose. It began in a temple with an inquisitive adolescent who didn't follow His parents home. Where will it begin for you? And when it does, will you, like Mary, recognize that your child is increasing in "wisdom and stature" (v. 52)—and begin the tough process of *letting go*?

FIFTEEN

SOME THINGS NEVER CHANGE

MARY KNEW TO STAY CONNECTED

On the third day there was a wedding in Cana of Galilee, and the mother of Jesus was there.

—JOHN 2:1

Eighteen years pass between the story of young Jesus in the temple and the launching of His earthly ministry with His first miracle. By this time, Mary has fully matured into the mother of an adult child. According to Scripture, she is a widow, so her life has changed on many fronts. What hasn't changed is the love she has for her son or the stronghold of her faith as His life has progressed.

Mary has spent her entire motherhood waiting for this moment. No doubt she did not have all the details as to when God would call Jesus to begin His earthly ministry. Like any mother whose child is setting out to embrace his or her passion and destiny, she must have experienced anticipation, excitement, and concern for her firstborn son. The comfort Mary had was the knowledge and faith that God would lead Jesus through each step of His journey.

When the story of the wedding feast begins, we see that Mary is in attendance. Jesus and His disciples are also in Cana to enjoy this celebration. We know this wedding was a rather large event because it was overseen by an event coordinator, better known as a master of the banquet. In that era, much like this one, someone who would pay attention to the details handled big events so the family could experience the fullness of the event without worry or concern. One detail, however, slipped through the cracks: there isn't enough wine for all the guests. Before long, there's none at all.

It is at this point of the story that we see Mary acting like a mother. She is a very observant woman who has paid attention to details since the beginning of her role as Jesus' mother. Like most moms, she is noticing the events of the evening and recognizes that a problem has arrived for the groom. It is a disaster if a wedding party runs out of wine, and she feels compelled to tell her son.

> We may not always understand the decisions, choices, or timing of our children's actions.

Jesus' response to his mother has puzzled people for years. In some ways it sounds as if He is chastising her for bringing the issue to Him. Yet, when He speaks to her, He refers to His mother with a term of intimacy: "dear woman" (John 2:4 NIV). He knew something she did not know, but all He could do in that moment was comfort her with those words and tell her that the timing was not right. What an important lesson for mothers of adult children to embrace: we may not always understand the decisions, choices, or timing of our children's actions.

Parenting adult children is very different from parenting in the earlier years. Mothers often find this season stressful because when their children mature, they can no longer relate to them from a position of power, control, or authority over their children's lives. This transition can be difficult because the relationship inevitably takes unanticipated turns.

Mary Is Always a Mother

Letting go is one of the most difficult challenges a mother faces. It is in her nature to protect, defend, and instruct her children. There comes a point, however, when she has to step back and reframe the way she mothers her adult children. Her continued success in their relationship will be partly dependent on her ability to adapt to their way of processing life and respect their right to explore and find their way through various challenges, yet still remain connected. While everything inside of her may want to regress to her earlier ways, it will be the wise mother who recognizes the importance of this new chapter for both of them.

Mary and Jesus were able to walk through this season well because they had developed a close, trusting relationship. They were confident in each other's motives and heart. They recognized that they might see things differently, but each never doubted who the other was or questioned the other's love. In fact, we see Mary approaching Jesus as an adult who is totally capable and ready to embrace His role.

Mary Respects Her Son

One of the key lessons in this passage of Scripture focuses on Mary's interaction with Jesus. Not only do we see her turning to

Him in the middle of a crisis, but also we see that the attitude with which she treats Him is clearly respectful.

Some people might say, "What is not to respect? Of course she respects Him. He is the Son of God." Yet the lesson is not simply about Jesus being the Son of God, but about Jesus being Mary's son. She would never forget His role as the future Messiah, but equally significant to her was her relationship with Him as His mother. At the core of her being, she was His mother first, and He would be her Savior later.

Throughout this story, Mary is respectful toward her son. Her attitude, tone of voice, and style of communicating demonstrates how important it is for mothers to remain respectful toward their children. This is often a difficult concept for mothers to grasp, since they believe they deserve respect regardless of their attitude. For most mothers, simply being a mother is worthy of their children's respect.

As love must first be experienced before it can be shared, so, too, must respect. When adults have demonstrated respect to children by listening to them and taking them seriously, they have communicated to their children that they are of great value. Likewise, respected children will most often grow up to be respectful. Of course, there may be moments when this is not the case or even developmental phases where we see the "respect" factor tumble slightly. At the core of the relationship, however, will be a foundation where mutual respect will be the underpinning that will allow the connection to endure and strengthen the relationship.

Young adults long to be respected by their parents. More

than anything in the world, they want their parents to approve of who they are. There will be times when their actions may not be worthy of your blessing because they do not line up with your personal values or convictions. What should never change, however, is your ability to be loving and respectful, even if it is in the midst of establishing strict boundaries.

> If I treat others, including my children, without respect, then it is time for me to examine my heart.

What most parents fail to recognize is that our response to our adult children is just that: *our* response. The way we interact is about our integrity and who we are, not about our children. What comes out of our mouths is solely about us and has nothing to do with anyone else. If I lose it because I am disappointed or angry, then I need to deal with how I feel. If I treat others, including my children, without respect, then it is time for me to examine my heart.

Mary Had Confidence in Her Son

Another valuable lesson from Mary is her belief in who Jesus was and what He could do. Mary had a very clear understanding of His purpose because God had spoken to her before He was conceived and told her why Jesus was being born. It is a gift she received at the beginning of His existence and it gave her a laser focus on how she would parent Him. It also gave her perspective on the importance of her role in His life.

Most mothers will not have a clear and specific purpose for their children when they are born. What they can have, however, is a focused and intentional purpose for their motherhood.

> Every woman can determine the type of mom she wants to be and set the course for the journey.

Every woman can determine the type of mom she wants to be and set the course for the journey. Knowing that each child is important and unique, a mom can embrace her children with confidence that God has entrusted her with them. Her role will exist throughout her entire life.

When Mary brought the empty wine jars to Jesus, she was fully confident in His ability to address the problem. She didn't know it was going to be His first miracle. She just knew she could count on Him to solve the problem in some way. She simply believed in Him.

Many of today's parents struggle to believe in their adult children. Maybe it is because of prior mistakes. In some cases, it can be associated with a long history of disappointment. Whatever the reason, mothers who struggle to believe that God can work through their children need to adjust their faith. Our crisis of confidence is really about our lack of trust that the God who created them can actually do something productive through them and with them.

Many times young adults struggle with having self-confidence. They may have made bad decisions before, and they know they have already messed up. Thus, when they are trying to turn their lives around to make better choices, they are fearful that they will mess up again. The last thing they want to hear is an "I told you so" from the one who knows them best.

When mothers can communicate confidence to their offspring, it is very empowering and freeing. It tells their adult children that they are not being held to the limitations of the past, but to the new opportunity today brings. Young adults will often hold on to their mother's confidence until they can develop some of their own.

Mothers of all ages and stages need to recognize the power they possess and the hope they can bring to a child who is attempting to discover his purpose, redeem her past, or find hope for the future. They have been given an amazing and unique position to impact the course their children are on. All it takes is the willingness to step outside of what they see and embrace this time as a gift where faith foots the bill. It is very important for mothers to remember that they cannot place the burden of hope in the wisdom of their children, but must place it in the hands of their Creator. Keeping their focus on their faith will prohibit them from placing undue pressure on their children, allowing them to be peaceful regardless of the path their children are traveling.

This story ends with Jesus performing His first miracle and His mother being there to see it happen. What a gift this must have been for her! It is yet another confirmation of who Jesus is and the world finally getting to see manifested what Mary has known all along. Her confidence and faith had paid off, and she would now be free to experience her son on a completely new level.

Mothering adult children is a challenge to everything moms have experienced. Yet this story of Mary and Jesus at this season of His adulthood encourages us to pay attention to who we are and the faith we possess. We will not be able to control our children's choices at that age, nor will we always agree with the decisions they make. But that is not our job. We have been given the opportunity to embrace our role with faith, respect, and honor. When we see this season as one that calls for faith instead of expectations, then the door opens for us to have more peace, to communicate our hope, to rest in the knowledge that there is someone who loves them more than we do, and to simply stay connected.

SIXTEEN

HOLDING ON WHEN THE DARKNESS COMES

MARY KNEW TO TRUST GOD WITH ALL THINGS
AND WITH HER CHILD

*Now there stood by the cross of Jesus His mother,
and His mother's sister, Mary the wife of Clopas,
and Mary Magdalene.*

—JOHN 19:25

nguish. There is not a better word in the English language to describe this moment in Mary's life. Although Mary knew all along that the time would come when her heart would be pierced over Jesus' suffering and death, the knowledge would not make the pain any less and the sadness any lighter. She is witnessing her son's slow execution and places herself at His side in the world's darkest hour.

Mary probably had witnessed the mock trial, where Jesus was sentenced to die a cruel and unjustified death. She had seen His disciples flee, lacking courage and faith when challenged to testify about their relationship with Him. She even may have witnessed the horrible beatings He endured, watching

> Although Mary knew her heart would be pierced over Jesus' suffering and death, the knowledge would not make the pain any less and the sadness any lighter.

pools of blood flow from His broken body. Could there be any greater horror for a mother to experience?

Jesus' life was completely out of her hands and in the Father's. There was absolutely nothing she could do to comfort or rescue her son. She had no idea how long His suffering would go on, and no doubt she had to battle the conflict in her heart.

As the mother of Jesus, Mary was overcome with grief and sadness. He had once been her baby boy, whom she had cradled in her arms and held close to her bosom. She witnessed Him take His first steps, and later watched Him explore the world with all the curiosity a two-year-old can muster.

Jesus had been her little boy, whom she had spent endless hours loving, teaching, and equipping for life. She had watched Him as He played with other children and learned the carpentry trade from His earthly father, Joseph.

Mary had walked alongside Jesus as He entered His manhood and studied the Scriptures with the temple rabbis. Being the thinking mother we know her to be, she undoubtedly engaged in hearty discussions with Jesus about biblical history, the cultural issues of the day, and the kingdom of God. She knew Him well, probably better than any other human.

Holding On When Her Heart Is Breaking

Now we see Mary at the cross, weeping over her son's impending death. She knew Jesus was bigger than life as well as death. She knew God's plan, Jesus' purpose, and her role. She was selected by God Himself to be the mother of His Son, and she would be there to the very end. Although three other women accompanied her, this painful and difficult moment could not be equally shared.

Just when it seems as if Jesus' plight could not get any worse, those who are within earshot of Him behold a tender encounter, just before His death. Of all the things He could have concerned Himself with, He makes His mother His priority.

> Mary knew
> God's plan,
> Jesus' purpose,
> and her role.

Jesus, in a faint and weakening voice, calls out to His mother: "Dear woman . . ." (John 19:26 NIV). This was a term of intimacy that He used with His mom; His calling out to her in this way reminded her of her importance to her son. Mothers cherish moments like this because they reveal the depth of the relationship between mom and child. This was one of those times that Mary would ponder as she reflected on her last treasured moments with Jesus.

Jesus' remaining words to His mother reflect His sense of responsibility to care for the woman He loved so deeply. "Here is your son" is a declaration to Mary that He is transferring her care over to the disciple He most trusted. Jesus wanted her to know that He would not leave her to fend for herself, but to be cared for and loved by someone He knew would love her as if she were his own mother.

Since Joseph had died, Mary's care would have fallen upon the firstborn son. Thus, Jesus cares for His mother to the very end by making sure she will be loved and honored after He is gone.

Jesus takes the transfer of relationship to its final step when He tells John that Mary is now *his* mother. This declaration communicates to John his new responsibilities to Mary, as well as the love and loyalty he is to show her. John trusted Jesus implicitly, and Jesus knew He could count on John to love His mother the way John had loved Him. In creating this bond for Mary and John, Jesus gave them more than a responsibility; He gave them each a new relationship where memories could be shared, hope could be encouraged, and faith could be embraced.

> When Mary faces her most difficult moment as a mother, she is found present and faithful to her child. Most important, she is found faithful to God, the Father.

When Mary faces her most difficult moment as a mother, she is found present and faithful to her child. Most important, she is found faithful to God, the Father.

Difficulty often causes women to struggle with trusting God. Fear sets in, hopelessness weighs heavy, and anger surfaces because the life they longed for, or the decision they hoped would pan out, has been lost in the unexpected realities of life. When a child dies, divorce strikes, a job is lost, or grandchildren rebel, the core beliefs of a woman's faith are tested. *What does it all mean? Does God really love me? Does He really love my children?*

Crises force people to make decisions about what they

believe and in whom they trust. A woman has to decide what she will do with her faith when her heart is breaking. This decision will impact the way she copes, the path she will take, and whether hope is a part of her future.

I recently heard a mother speak about the loss of her child. Her son had died tragically in a car accident, and it had been less than a year since his death. She shared that in the early days after his death, she could not see any possibility of ever finding hope or purpose again. As time went by, she realized that her despair was not reflecting well on the life her son had lived. She decided she would once again embrace life to the fullest because it would be the best way to honor his legacy and keep his impact alive. In other words, she made a decision to live again.

Love invites us to live in the midst of darkness. Sometimes it has to be done a second at a time, but the invitation for mothers is to choose faith. Anguish will be experienced and loss must be grieved, but the process will not be permanent because love will win due to the sustaining and enduring nature of God's faithfulness. Whatever a mother is asked to relinquish, even if it is her child, God understands her pain and sorrow because He has been there. He never asks mothers to go to a place He Himself has not gone.

Trusting in the Midst of Suffering

The ultimate form of trust is when we release the outcome of our lives into God's hands. The same is equally true for moms and their children's futures. Whether a child is two months old, twenty-two years old, or over fifty, a mother will always see that child as one she is to love, protect, and outlive. When life changes that expectation, something deeper with purpose and meaning must replace it. The only answer that has consistently sufficed has been a personal faith in the Christ who died and rose again. Nothing else has been able to cause the weak to stand, the brokenhearted to testify, and the empty life to be full again.

> The ultimate form of trust is when we release the outcome of our lives into God's hands.

Years ago, I was asked to speak at a holiday banquet in November. The group wanted me to address "what happens when God chooses not to heal." I was taken aback by their choice of such a dire topic, especially since this was to be held before Thanksgiving. Nonetheless, I accepted the invitation and immediately began praying about what I would possibly share.

I became curious about the topic and sensed there had to be a reason it had been selected. I decided to query the women's ministry director about what particular areas they wanted me to address.

"We have four mothers in our congregation and school community who have malignant diseases or conditions who will probably not be with us this time next year. Our ladies are struggling with the pain and loss these women and their families are experiencing. I thought we needed to hit the issue head-on so we can help the entire church more effectively deal with the pain," said Janice. I admired her courage and respected her willingness to step into an uncomfortable place.

As I prayed, God took me to the passage in John 9 where the man is born blind and the disciples ask Jesus if the man's blindness is the result of the man's sin, or the sin of his parents.

> As he went along, he saw a man blind from birth. His disciples asked him, "Rabbi, who sinned, this man or his parents, that he was born blind?"
>
> "Neither this man nor his parents sinned," said Jesus, "but this happened so that the works of God might be displayed in his life." (John 9:1–3 NIV)

Three hundred ladies showed up for this wonderful evening. I told them God had shown me in this story that the purpose of suffering is for people to know God at a deeper level and that when people suffer, He is giving them the privilege of being a reflection of Him to others who may not know Him. While no one volunteers for suffering, those who find themselves in that place have an opportunity to find value and meaning in it so it will not be in vain.

That event still stands out to me as the one where I was the most nervous. I usually do not feel anxiety, because I really enjoy communicating and speaking. But I knew there were dying people in the audience, and I did not want to add to their pain. Afterward, I sat down and prayed that the message had been received with the heart it had been given.

In a matter of thirty minutes, all four of the women who

were dying approached me and thanked me for the message. In every case, they said that while they did not want to leave their children, family, and friends, they could take comfort in knowing God would use their experience and story for His honor and glory. They felt they could face the future with greater peace knowing others could be blessed by their journey. Are you facing hardships—even life-threatening ones—whose eternal value seems vague in light of the immediate darkness? Faith is shaken to the core in these moments, and we have all experienced or witnessed them to some degree. What Mary shows us is that faith in our God is the bedrock of assurance in all things. That can never be taken away from us—it is a priceless gift that, if you nurture it well, can never erode.

> Mary shows us that faith in our God is the bedrock of assurance in all things.

Mary also shows us in her relationship with Jesus that a mother's job is never complete. Mothers want to be found faithful to the very end, to be loving mothers to our children, regardless of the circumstances we might find ourselves in, and faithful to the very Christ whose death saves us and gives us an eternal home with God. There is no higher act of love and devotion toward God and toward others than to clutch our faith in the Father when all seems lost. And there is no greater act for a mother than to trust God completely with her child, even when darkness comes.

SEVENTEEN

THE IMPORTANCE OF STAYING CONNECTED TO GOD

MARY KNEW TO BE A WOMAN OF PRAYER

*These all continued with one accord in prayer
and supplication, with the women and Mary the
mother of Jesus, and with His brothers.*

—ACTS 1:14

We have walked with Mary throughout the course of her journey as a woman and mother, and now, in the book of Acts, we find her at the place where she began: without a son and waiting for the Holy Spirit. Up until now, her story could be like many mothers' throughout the centuries. She had a son who was written off as a ne'er-do-well and a nobody. The difference between Mary and all other moms is in the verse above, in which Mary is found waiting for the Holy Spirit to arrive after her son Jesus has been resurrected from the dead. No other mother in all of history can claim this moment.

The previous forty-three days had encompassed man's lowest point and heaven's greatest gain. Mary had endured the agony of her son's death, the grief of the tomb, and had celebrated the miracle of the resurrection. For forty days she had witnessed His presence among His disciples, including John, the one to whom Jesus had entrusted her care. (He was now one of the main leaders among them and would be a part of Christ's postresurrection encounters.)

Can you imagine her gratitude and excitement? Mary had seen her resurrected son with her own eyes, and hope had returned, not only for her as a mother, but also for the whole world. Mary must have felt a myriad of feelings: joy, relief, hope, anticipation, and validation. She had been doubted, estranged, and misunderstood, much as her son had for most of His life. She had lived with the knowledge of His identity long before anyone else would grasp who He was. Now she could live with a renewed confidence that her son had rightfully taken His place as the Savior of the world.

Although Jesus had returned in a supernatural form, Mary did not care. She was simply elated that He had been among them and had demonstrated His divine Sonship to His followers and skeptics alike. Although Jesus had ascended into heaven perhaps just hours before the time described in this verse, she knew this was just another step in the eternal journey for her son. No doubt, Mary's selfless heart took over because she knew Jesus was finally with the very Father who had created Him and graciously shared Him with her.

Thus, as we examine the last recorded act of Mary's life, her legacy is finalized because she models for all women and moms the secret of her sustaining faith: she is a woman of prayer.

It seems so simple. In fact, it is so simple it is overlooked, underpracticed, and barely recognized for the power source that it is. Even in Mary's story, this part of her faith is rarely acknowledged in pulpits and Bible studies. Yet her example as a participant waiting for the coming of the Holy Spirit speaks volumes about her understanding the gift that was to come from her son.

Mary Recognized the Source of Her Strength

Prior to the coming of the Holy Spirit, God would grant impartations of His Spirit for moments or limited amounts of time for a divine and holy purpose to be accomplished. Throughout the Old Testament, we also see supernatural moments that could only be accounted for as some divine presence from heaven. The burning bush, the pillar of fire, and the parting of the Red Sea are just a few examples where God divinely stepped in to guide and protect His people. This history was Mary's foundation of faith when the angel appeared to her at the very beginning of her motherhood journey.

Because of her familiarity with the Holy Spirit's work in her life as the mother of Christ, she is found in Acts waiting with faithfulness for the permanent gift that was to come to all people who believe in her son. Of those who could testify to its magnificence, Mary could speak most loudly of its blessing and strength. It is because of this special gift that she endured the journey as Jesus' mother with grace, honor, and faith.

Mary is also seen waiting for this special gift because she understood that the journey was not over and the work of the kingdom was entering a whole new level. She appreciated how transforming the Spirit had been in her own life and understood that God's plan for the ages was to include the birth of His presence in a way that would change the world.

Mary's role in this verse continues as a stalwart of faith even as she's the mother of Jesus. It also makes reference to her other sons, even though they are not the ones who are caring for her in her last days. That assignment had been given to John, the beloved disciple and friend of Jesus. Thus, her motherhood would still need a divine presence as she lived out her life with her other children.

We could all greatly benefit from the divine presence we call the Holy Spirit. Unfortunately, He is not a well-known aspect of God's presence because we have made Him too mystical to be practical. If women recognized Him as the helpmate and partner He is, we could step into a new, powerful facet of faith and intimacy with God. This divine partner could lead families worldwide into greater love, closer ties, and better communication.

> This divine partner {the Holy Spirit} could lead families worldwide into greater love, closer ties, and better communication.

Throughout my years working with women, I have noticed that *peace* is the common missing ingredient among all women. Restless nights and endless stress fill a woman's heart when she is left empty because she simply has no answers. Anxiety-filled moms are everywhere you turn, whether their children are young or old, healthy or dysfunctional, faith-filled or faithless. Like any woman, mothers struggle with peace when they do not have answers to the issues their children face. Wouldn't it be great if we could embrace the same source of peace and power that Mary did as she encountered the trials of her faith and her motherhood?

Being a woman of prayer does not mean we sit in a perpetual

state of closed eyes and bowed heads. There are moments when that posture is appropriate and needed. We need to be more frequently and naturally connected to the source of our strength, however, if we are to make prayer a relationship with the One who loves our children and us more than we can conceive. A relationship is a two-way street and prayer is a two-way conversation, where talking and listening are a part of the experience, and can take place anywhere, anytime, and in any situation.

I have prayed in doctor's offices and bathroom stalls. I have prayed in the car and on a plane. I have talked to God in a loud voice when I am frustrated and upset. I have whispered my secrets when I desperately needed to tell Him of my broken heart. Regardless of the moment or the topic, I have been real and honest. I haven't played games or used religious words. I needed help and strength in the midst of my motherhood journey, and I have not been afraid to put my heart out there for Him to see how badly I needed Him.

God has met me in those difficult places and has answered prayers few thought He would answer. Sometimes He made me wait until He had put all the pieces in place so He could give me His best answer. Sometimes He has said no when I made a request, but only

> The angel was not kidding when he told Mary that "nothing is impossible with God."

because He had a better *yes* in store. During those seasons of accepting an answer I did not want or understand, I grew in my trust and faithfulness to Him. He never wasted a moment, even though there were times I was not pleased when an answer did not arrive in the timing I had hoped for. Regardless of my need, request, or despair, God was with me and I was never alone.

When mothers use the power available to them because they are trusting God for their strength and wisdom, things happen and lives change. The angel was not kidding when he told Mary that "nothing is impossible with God." I have seen God do the impossible in my family as well as families all across this country, and I have no doubt God longs to do it more, if only He were invited to do so.

Mary Was Faithful to the End

If the Son of God finds the need to be personal and vulnerable with God, wouldn't it make sense that women need to approach Him on their own behalf?

It is very encouraging to see Mary still being faithful once her role as the mother of Jesus is no longer needed. What this tells mothers is that she had learned to be dependent on God because she needed Him as a woman, not just as a mother. This is an important truth every woman needs to embrace.

Too often we call on God because of our concerns, especially those of our children. While this is wonderful and good, the woman's impact will be limited if she is not practicing her faith for herself. Jesus Himself spent time alone with God, discussing His needs and asking His questions. If the Son of God finds the need to be personal and vulnerable with God, wouldn't it make sense that women need to approach Him on their own behalf?

Mary is found waiting for the Holy Spirit to come, not because she is the mother of Jesus, but because she wants to have access to all of God that she can receive. She is doing this for herself, and her hope is that God will reveal more of Himself through this perpetual presence known as the Holy Spirit. She had faith to believe that God could use her as a witness to her world, which would also encompass becoming a part of the birthing of the church. She recognized that while her role may have changed, her opportunity to bless the kingdom was still alive and growing.

It would be a wonderful gift to today's adults if their mothers recognized the importance of maintaining their faith after their children have left home. Some of the most damaging and difficult stories I hear have come from children whose faith was pulled out from under them when they witnessed their parents depart from the faith they had preached to their kids their entire lives.

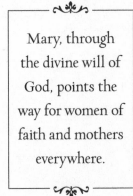

> Mary, through the divine will of God, points the way for women of faith and mothers everywhere.

Our influence, our power to impact, and our legacy are on the line until the last breath in our bodies. Mary, through the divine will of God, despite the theological battleground she has become, points the way for women of faith and mothers everywhere. Women can never assume their influence is diminished or insignificant to those around them, including their children

> A woman who draws her strength from prayer will find meaning and purpose regardless of her role or circumstances.

and families. The witness and legacy of our faith witness will ring long and loud long after we are gone. A woman who draws her strength from prayer will find meaning and purpose regardless of her role or circumstances. Most important, by staying connected with God, she will leave a legacy of peace and will be a powerful reflection of God's love and presence in her life.

EPILOGUE

In the opening chapter, I shared how I wanted to be chosen to play the role of Mary when I was a little girl. What I realized in writing this book is that God did choose me. He didn't want me to play a role, but He wanted me to experience the mystical and divine privilege of knowing Him. And part of that journey came through being a mother. By giving me children, He gave me the same blessing that He gave to Mary, a unique way to know Him on an intimate level, as Mary did.

This blessing, however, wasn't just for me. It is for you too. It is for any woman who will allow her heart to be totally entrusted into the hands of God. He gave us Mary as an example so we would know that motherhood can be done well in the midst of impossible circumstances. He also knew that shining the spotlight on Mary's motherhood would be a way for Him to bring attention to your own parenting.

When we began the journey of this book, we knew Mary as a virgin, a wife, and a mother to Jesus. Now we can see more clearly the depth of who she is and was, and why God chose her to be the greatest mother who ever lived. Thus, three roles surface on which every mother can reflect:

As a Child of God

In the beginning of Mary's life, we see her relating to God simply as His child. She was authentic in her responses and willing in her heart. Although she had no clue what her *yes* to the angel would mean, she knew she could trust God to be faithful to her without her having all the answers or knowing His plan.

Mary's relationship with God at this stage of her life was that of a trusting daughter. She believed what He said and took Him at His word. He told her to "fear not" and He would be with her. Throughout her life, she would maintain the trust a loving daughter can have in her heavenly Father.

As a Mother

Mary understood that Jesus was the Son of God, but she first knew Him as *her* son. She was a mother first and recognized the importance of paying attention to her son's life. She knew she could not control the events of His life, but she could take responsibility for how she mothered Him.

Mary recognized her role in Christ's life and did all she could to be the mother Jesus needed her to be. What she could not do was rescue Him, protect Him from His destiny, or change the course of His life, and stay faithful to her relationship with God.

As a Woman

Ultimately, the cherished people in our lives and our children learn from who we are, not what we do. We are teachers and role models for faith and everything female and feminine. In fact, for our children we define their normal for all things female, and they will compare all other women to us. This is an important thought that we need to recognize and embrace if we are going to be true to ourselves.

We need to see ourselves from God's perspective because it will greatly impact the influence we have on the most important people in our lives. Our words about our faith will ring hollow to our children if we do not embrace our value with the honor and respect God gives us as His daughters. It is important for us to realize that the value we place on ourselves reflects the value we place on our relationship with Christ.

So Where Do We Go from Here?

Every woman has a story, but most of us have not stepped back to reflect on what our story might be. Just as Mary's life unfolded, your life is unfolding in full view of those around you and, if you're a mother, in the presence of your children. Whether they are young or old, what they are learning from you is what will stay with them long after you are gone.

As important as your children are, what will really matter in the end is who you believe you are as a woman and how that forms your motherhood. Becoming a woman who fully trusts the Lord and leaning into the journey of motherhood will reveal many imperfections and weaknesses. But as we learned from Mary, any journey worth taking is more about who God is for us rather than our shortcomings. If you take away anything from this book, may it be this: Mary trusted and followed her heavenly Father who called her to be the mother of Jesus and equipped her for it. If you find yourself wondering whether you have a personal relationship with Christ, now is the moment to settle this question.

Whatever you do as a woman or as a mom, never forget that trust and obedience is paramount. As mothers, never for one second forget that you were meant to be the mother of your children at this time in this place. It is a divine appointment, a charge given to you by God. No other woman will ever be as important to your children as you. How you decide to handle this truth will shape your parenting from this generation forward. Remember, motherhood is as much about you as it will ever be about your children.

Let's join our hearts together as women and mothers so we can shake the rafters of the kingdom because we believe God will be to us what He was to Mary.

ABOUT THE AUTHOR

Catherine Hickem, LCSW, a licensed psychotherapist with three decades of experience, is a relationship expert who has made it her life's mission to equip women for every facet of their lives. As a minister's daughter, minister's wife, and women's ministry leader in church, she has spoken at hundreds of women's events and has spent her entire adult life working with women of all ages and in all stages of life.

Hickem's newsletter, website, seminars, retreats, and resources reach thousands with practical tips on all issues facing women. She is also the author of *Regret Free Parenting*, where she offers seven powerful principles for mothers to raise their children well . . . and be confident they're doing it right

Catherine lives with her husband, Neil, in Delray Beach, Florida. She has two grown children, Taylor and Tiffany, as well as a niece, Lindsay, who with her husband, John, and daughter, Maggie, she claims as her own. She has offices in South Florida and Metro Atlanta.

ACKNOWLEDGMENTS

I would like to thank the following people who have contributed to making this book come alive:

My family, Neil, Taylor, and Tiffany, who are often the object of my stories and allow me to share our journey with the world. I especially want to thank you, Tiffany, for helping birth the title. How sweet of God to give you that revelation!

Don Jacobson, whose confidence in me is truly humbling and who has been so much more than an agent and has become a friend, mentor, and spiritual ally.

Barry Baird, the person God used to intervene in my literary journey and who has blessed me with his support, friendship, and kindness.

Bryan Norman, the editor of a lifetime, whom I enjoy as a friend and respect greatly as the wonderful professional he is.

Sami Cone, whose assistance in helping me process Mary's story allowed me to have clarity and bring the voice to her life that would allow women to learn from her.

To my ministry team—past and present—Lynn Van Lenten, Lindsay Mardick, Mary Peat, Cynthia Seely—you are so committed to teaching Mary's story of faith to mothers and women. Thank you for your love and support day after day.

The Mary Book Prayer Team—Dusty Allison, Cindy Barber, Carrie Bayhan, Fitz Carty, Marsha Crowe, Chela DiMura, Jerilyn Ewton, Lynn Fisher, Carol Ann Gushue, Susan Hagen, Vanessa Hewko, Renee Kennedy, Jeanette Lewis, Rebecca Nelson, Martha Luzinski, Paula Martinez, Diana Masullo, Judy McMillan, Jackie Perez, Suzanne Souder, Rebecca Scott, Dorinda Spahr, Pat Stacy, Holly Schuttler, Suzanne Williams— who have taken to heart the message of faith through Mary's life and the potential to impact women everywhere. Thank you for praying for me as well as praying for every reader who picks up this book.

All the wonderful people of Thomas Nelson who feel like friends, not just business colleagues. It is truly an honor to partner with each of you.

Most important, God, for revealing Mary's story to me so women could have a human example of what faith and love can look like in a woman who is totally faithful to her God.

AN INVITATION . . .

Throughout the course of the book Mary models for us what it means to have a personal relationship with God. When Christ came into the world, it was the answer for mankind's human condition. For us to have the intimacy with God that Mary did, all of us must come into an understanding of our need for Him and recognize what He has done for us. Let me share a few thoughts for you to consider if you are interested in knowing God the way she did.

First, we need to know how much He truly loves us. Jeremiah 31:3 says, *"I have loved you, my people, with an everlasting love.*

With unfailing love I have drawn you to myself" (NLT). God wants us to know His love is real, unending, and sacrificial.

Second, we need to understand the nature and condition in which we find ourselves. *"For everyone has sinned; we all fall short of God's glorious standard"* (Romans 3:23 NLT). All of us make mistakes and think of things that do not reflect a perfect God. In other words, we are imperfect beings who need a relationship with a perfect God.

Third, God wants to deliver us from our sinful condition and give the gift of spending eternity with Him. Romans 6:23 says, *"For the wages of sin is death, but the free gift of God is eternal life through Christ Jesus our Lord"* (NLT).

Fourth, eternal life and salvation come through faith in Jesus Christ. *"For God loved the world so much that he gave his one and only Son, so that everyone who believes in him will not perish but have eternal life"* (John 3:16 NLT). This amazing gift to you and me comes at a high price to Him but is free to us who believe. We cannot earn it nor do we deserve it. *"God saved you by his grace when you believed. And you can't take credit for this; it is a gift from God"* (Ephesians 2:8 NLT).

Last, your invitation is this: pray the prayer on the next page and ask Christ to become your Lord and Savior. When you pray this, you are becoming a child of God and will have the promise of eternity with Him. *"If you confess with your mouth that Jesus is Lord and believe in your heart that God raised him from the dead, you will be saved. For it is by believing in your heart that you are made right with God, and it is by confessing with your mouth that you are saved"* (Romans 10:9–10 NLT).

Pray a prayer like this:

Dear God, thank You for loving me and making it possible to have my sins forgiven. I admit that I sin and have made mistakes. I know, however, that You have forgiven me and made it possible for me to experience Your grace on earth and eternal life in heaven. I believe Jesus Christ is the Son of God and paid the price for my sins by dying on the cross. I believe that He rose from the grave and lives forever. I accept Him as my Lord and Savior, and gladly receive Your free gift of spending eternity with You. Thank You, Father, for hearing my prayer and forgiving my sins, and securing a place for me in heaven. I pray this in Your name, amen.

If you prayed this prayer and want to know more on growing in your relationship with Christ, e-mail me at catherinehickem@ bellsouth.net and I will send you more information on growing in your faith. I pray blessings on you for making the most important decision in your life.

Catherine

THE PONDER
MOVEMENT

I n this book, you have had an opportunity to see what
God could do with a woman who took time to reflect
on Him, herself, her relationships, and her priorities. No
doubt we have learned the value of what happens when a woman
chooses to keep the truly important things at the forefront of
her thought life. What do you think would happen in your life
if you made a decision to ponder more frequently?

If you are ready to begin a journey of pondering, then log
on to www.CatherineHickem.com and begin the process of

taking your thought life to a deeper level. There is a special section designed for women who long to arrive at the end of their lives with a full heart, grateful spirit, meaningful relationships, and as few regrets as possible. Most of all, you will have the opportunity to know God in a more intimate way.

If you have learned something from *Heaven in Her Arms* that has impacted you, let us hear from you. E-mail us at PonderMovement@CatherineHickem.com so we can celebrate your new insights and awareness.

Ponder on,
Catherine

HEAVEN IN HER ARMS STUDY GUIDE

BY CATHERINE HICKEM, LCSW

Chapters 1-3

Key Verses: Luke 1:26, 30-32

As we have seen thus far, Mary comes from a heritage that was anything but royal. Her family did not possess wealth, power, or influence. In fact, they lived in a community that was known to be lowly and poor. No doubt this was not the background anyone expected God to select to be the home of a king.

Expectations. They are often a roadblock for women and their faith. They become like cement because our minds and hearts get hardened and they prevent us from having miraculous moments in our lives. We get stuck with believing there is one way for God to answer our prayer or meet our need. As a result, we limit God from revealing Himself in a more powerful way through us.

Mary's selection as the woman God would choose to be the mother of His Son would not line up with the Jewish faithful and government leaders.

1. What do you believe the Jews expected to be the background of their Messiah? Describe those expectations.

....

....

....

2. Mary was only about fourteen at the time the angel appeared to her. What made her different from most teenage girls her age? Identify her areas of maturity.

....

....

....

3. As you think on Mary, reflect on what type of mother she must have had. What type of relationship do you think they had?

....

....

....

4. What evidence do we have in the Scripture that tells us Mary has courage? Share your insights on this truth.

....

....

....

5. The angel tells Mary twice to not be fearful. Fear is probably the biggest obstacle that prevents women from having profound experiences in their faith. What do we need to know in our hearts to possess the faith Mary demonstrated when her journey began?

....

....

....

6. What if you were Mary's mom? How do you think you would have handled it? What lessons can you learn from this reflection that encourages you?

....

....

....

Chapters 4-6

Key Verses: Luke 4:33-38

In these chapters, we begin to see who Mary is and how she thinks. Upon hearing the angel's pronouncement of her future, she boldly asks a question that is both logical and curious. Since she was a virgin, she wanted to know how this miraculous event was going to take place. Wouldn't any woman want an answer to that question? Knowing this event could cost her life, Mary faces it with courage.

The angel responds to Mary's inquiry by giving her the answer every woman for all of time needs to hear. He tells her that she will raise the Son of God through God's supernatural presence, reinforcing she is not alone in the most unique role of all time. This promise of God's presence should be comforting to every woman regardless of what she is facing, because the answer that worked for Mary will work for all women who truly trust.

Upon completion of the angel's revelation, Mary reveals why God could trust her. She tells the angel that her life was not her own and she would do as God desired. In other words, she released Him of all her expectations so she could fulfill what He needed her to do. What an amazing act of obedience! Her confidence in who God is hits its crescendo in Mary's declaration and women are left with an example of total selflessness.

All three of these moments reveal tremendous insights into Mary's faith. They also surface opportunities for women of all ages and stages of life to reflect on their own journeys of trust.

1. In Luke 1:34, Mary questions the angel about her soon-to-be pregnant state. All of us will have questions we want to inquire of God, but if we are hesitant out of fear, it indicates we do not trust Him. How do you reconcile Mary's boldness

in her question to the angel with your courage to ask God the hard questions?

....

....

....

2. Can you think of a time in Jesus' life when He asks God a question? What does that mean for you and your faith?

....

....

....

3. In verse 35, the angel gives Mary the answer to her question. More important, he gives all women the answer to how they will face any challenges or crises in their lives. Read the verse again and share what that means to you.

....

....

....

4. The angel says to Mary, "Nothing is impossible with God." Why do you think he says this to Mary? Why do women have a difficult time believing this is true for them?

....

....

....

5. Mary addresses lordship in this verse (38). Her perspective gives us insight into a dimension of her faith's depth. How does this impact your understanding of her selflessness?

....

....

....

6. In verse 38, we have another insight as to why God selected Mary to be the mother of His Son. Upon hearing God's plan for her life, she relinquishes any of her expectations so she can be completely obedient to Him. What do you think caused her to walk in complete faith? Share with your group what God has showed you about this moment in Mary's life.

....

....

....

Chapters 7–9

Key Verses: Luke 1:39–55

Upon Mary's declaration of relinquishing her life, she immediately goes to her older cousin Elizabeth, who is experiencing a miracle of her own. This is a critical time in Mary's life because she is going to encounter many doubters, some of whom may be those closest to her. By going to Elizabeth, a mature and seasoned woman of faith, she will have the opportunity to be nurtured, mentored, and believed. Mary needed another woman in her life who could understand her journey, and God met her in that place of need.

Elizabeth is so excited to have the privilege of having Mary in her home. In the midst of her joy, she makes a very special pronouncement when she says it will be Mary's faith that will be her legacy. Elizabeth has spiritual maturity to understand what God truly honors in any woman's heart: their faith and confidence in Him. Even the baby in her womb senses the excitement.

Mary reveals the depth of her knowledge of God in this spiritual song of praise. She declares her humility and God's greatness as she speaks and acknowledges His goodness amid the depravity of man. We have to remember that Mary is a fourteen-year-old girl, but when we listen to her in this passage, we see spiritual wisdom and insight beyond her years. No doubt, we see another reason why God would choose her.

1. Can you imagine what Mary must have thought once the angel left? Would her family believe her? Her journey into the unexpected begins with a trip to her older, pregnant cousin. Why do you think Mary needed a mentor?

....

....

....

2. The verse says Mary went to Elizabeth with haste. What do you think this means?

....

....

....

3. Elizabeth's excitement at Mary's arrival at her home is a message to all women today. We have the opportunity for the presence of Christ to be a part of our lives on a daily basis, but too often we do not appreciate the significance of this gift. How can we be reminded to have a daily appreciation of God's presence in our lives?

....

....

....

4. Elizabeth tells Mary that her legacy will be her faith. Most of us have believed her legacy was her role as the mother of the Son of God. What does this revelation mean to you? How does it change the lessons you learn from Mary?

....

....

....

5. When Mary sings her song of praise, what do you learn about her?

....

....

....

6. Mary's song reveals so much about who she is and what she is like. Take a few minutes and reflect on her personality. We see that God selected a young woman who was no wilting flower, but a woman of strength who was filled with courage and prepared for the task. What lessons can we take away from this passage for today's families? For women?

....

....

....

Chapters 10–12

Key Verses: Luke 2:1–35

These are the most familiar verses about Mary. If we look deeper, we will see so much more to this story. Joseph takes Mary to be his wife upon her arrival back to Nazareth. It isn't long before they receive notice that they will have to travel to Joseph's hometown for a census. He takes his role seriously and knows he will need to protect her.

Mary's role as a mother unfolds in Scripture and we know she will play a crucial role in Jesus' life. There are elements to her role that are not discussed but can clearly be appreciated by any woman. One can only imagine how much Jesus stood out among His peers and what it meant to Mary to know that so few people understood Him. Her journey had to be lonely and, once again, she would need to take comfort in her God. Every woman can relate to the pain Mary must have felt and can have the same hope if they turn to her God.

It becomes apparent in these verses that God valued Mary's reflective heart and thinking mind. She recognizes the significance of who Jesus is after His birth and makes a note to capture it while focusing on what has just happened. One can imagine what Mary took in the night Jesus was born: Was it the birth experience itself and holding her son for the first time? Was it the appearance of angels singing from the heavens? No doubt her mind was flooded with moments she never wanted to forget.

Being a Jewish woman who followed Old Testament law, she knew Joseph and she would need to follow the temple laws as an act of obedience. They were charged with the responsibility of raising Jesus and to do it well would mean they would need to be good role models for Him. Equally important is the understanding that Mary would follow the laws because of her love for God. Her obedience came from a place of faith and trust.

1. Today's moms are not allowed to travel after their seventh month of pregnancy. Mary was in her last month when she had to leave with Joseph for the census. Where does faith come in at this moment in Mary's life? What if you were

Mary's sister? How would you have processed this through the filter of your faith?

....
....
....

2. Has it ever dawned on you that one of Mary's greatest challenges was raising a boy no one understood? What does this revelation mean to you?

....
....
....

3. Verse 19 says, Mary "pondered [things] in her heart." What does this verse mean to you? What does this say about Mary?

....
....
....

4. God loves women who think. What are the benefits of a thinking woman? Why does a woman who ponders please Him so? What do you need to change in order to be a pondering woman?

....
....
....

5. Mary had demonstrated an obedient heart from the beginning. We find her continuing her obedience as one of the first acts as Jesus' mom. How does God show up for her in this moment?

....

....

....

6. In today's culture, people and families are more isolated than ever before. A support system can change one's life. What do you need to do to strengthen your support system? What can you learn from what God did in Mary's life that He wants to do in yours?

....

....

....

Chapters 13–15

Key Verses: Luke 2:35–52, John 2:1–10

Simeon gives Mary a prophecy that reveals she will be a widow when she has to walk through the darkest times with Jesus. Can you imagine knowing the future would have difficult days and you would be humanly alone, without your spouse, to deal with the challenge? This is another moment where we are given the opportunity to look at Mary up close and see how she holds on to her faith.

As Jesus grows, He is becoming everything He was created to be. Jesus wanted to learn all He could about His Father, and the temple celebrations were opportunities for Him to sit among the most learned religious leaders. The event that takes place between Jesus and His parents allows us to recognize the significance of Mary's motherhood role and Jesus' relationship to His Father. No doubt for Mary, this was a terrifying moment, and once again we see the significance of her pondering heart.

When Jesus launches His earthly ministry, we see that Mary is present. She had waited for thirty years for this moment, and she had to be grateful His identity as the Son of God would now be revealed. This scripture is the first example we have of their relationship as adult to adult. Regardless of His majestic role, she still related to Him as her son. The focus of this passage is on the miracle, but the underlying story is between Mary and Jesus.

1. Verses 34–35 are often ignored in the Christmas story. Yet the truth of these scriptures is important for us to know. What significance do you believe these verses reveal?

....

....

....

2. So often people say they wish they knew the future. But what if the future revealed a dark time? How would your faith change to mentally and spiritually adapt to the difficult news?

....
....
....

3. Mary, Joseph, and Jesus went to the temple with great anticipation. The ending of the trip was chaotic. What did God
   want us to learn from this part of His Son's life? What does
   He want us to learn from Mary's life?

....
....
....

4. We learn that Mary once again "ponders" this most recent
   experience in the temple. What do you believe Mary thought
   about as she reflected on this experience? What lessons did
   she learn? Be prepared to share the last time you pondered
   something important to you and the lessons you learned.

....
....
....

5. The miracle at Cana is significant for many reasons. One of
   those reasons is that Jesus begins to fulfill the purpose of His
   creation. Think of this moment through Mary's eyes. What
   type of prayer do you think she prayed after the wedding was
   over and the first miracle was performed?

....
....
....

6. Parents of adult children often struggle to treat their adult
children like adults. What does Mary's role in this wedding
story say to you about her relationship with Jesus? What lessons do family members need to remember?

....
....
....

Chapters 16–Epilogue

Key Verses: John 19:25, Acts 1:14

This is a passage of Scripture in which we watch Mary
endure every mother's nightmare. She will have to walk alongside her son as He is abused and crucified. Like any good mother,
she is there to the very end, loving in whatever way she can. Her
anguish is deep and her presence is powerful. Most of all, her
faith continues to be steadfast. At the cross, we see Christ's finest moment and we observe a mother's darkest hour.

The next time we see Mary in Scripture is when she and
the disciples, as well as other believers, have gathered to wait
for the coming of the Holy Spirit. She is familiar with the
Spirit since thirty-three years earlier an angel had promised
her that the Holy Spirit would be with her. Her integrity of

faith continued to be a hallmark of Mary's character, faith, and spiritual wisdom.

As we have studied Mary's life, we have witnessed a woman whose faith was tested at every turn and she knew at every stage of her journey the source of her strength would be confidence in God. She knew Him well because she allowed Him to be an intimate part of her life that reflected a total dependency God desires for us all. This story invites each and every woman to ask the question: What part of my heart, spirit, mind, and soul do I need to turn over to Him to possess life-changing faith?

1. Mary could have stayed away during Jesus' last hours, but she was by His side as He experienced an excruciating death. How do you think she reconciled her anguish with her faith? When you find yourself in an impossible moment, what steps do you take that help you embrace your faith?

....

....

....

2. At the cross, Jesus cares for His mother by giving John responsibility for her care. What does that mean to you? What does it say about His relationship with His mother?

....

....

....

3. Christ had resurrected and returned to heaven to take His rightful place next to His father. Now His followers waited for the gift of the Holy Spirit to arrive so they could have a part of His presence with them at all times. Mary is found with the disciples, praying. What does this say about who Mary is?

....

....

....

4. Our last impression of Mary in Scripture focuses on her faithfulness to pray. What a marvelous legacy to leave! If Christ's mother made prayer a part of her life, what message does that send to every woman?

....

....

....

5. Mary is probably the most well-known woman in history. Her story has resonated with females across the years because we have related to some part of her story. You have a story and God is interested in being a part of your story. What inspiration do you take from Mary's life that motivates you to deepen your relationship with God? Be specific.

....

....

....

6. This is your moment to "ponder" who you are and what you want your faith legacy to be. Most of us will have to shed our fears, relinquish our control, and become less self-absorbed to live a life that reflects a faith that is alive, peaceful, and dependent of the Spirit of God. Take some time and write out a prayer that reflects a new work that God has done in your heart.

....

....

....

....

....

....

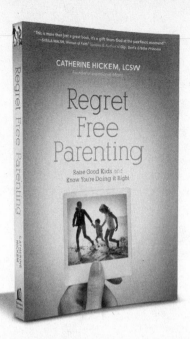

Also available from Catherine Hickem

Are my kids ready for the world? Did I teach them the right things? What if I made a bad decision that affects them forever? What could I have done differently?

Moms have a list of worries a mile long about their parenting. They fear they'll spend twenty years raising children—only to discover they missed investing in and teaching the things that mattered. How can any parent be sure she won't have regrets?

In *Regret Free Parenting: Raise Good Kids and Know You're Doing it Right*, acclaimed motherhood expert teaches the principles every mother needs to confidently raise her children. Catherine Hickem shows you how to:

- Build companionship and trust
- Live peacefully in the teen years
- Maintain your position as the parent
- Develop emotional intelligence
- Know the difference between control and intention
- And much, much more.

Most importantly, Hickem shows how to achieve intentional parenting. Everything important in life requires planning. And every mom knows her greatest legacy, the truest expression of her heart and hope for the world, is bound up in the way she raises her child. With a perspective rich in faith and tested by life, join Hickem and learn how you can achieve regret-free parenting!

"While mothering is the hardest job we'll ever undertake, our Creator designed it to be the most rewarding, most powerful, and closest to grasping God's heart."
—Catherine Hickem, LCSW

www.CatherineHickem.com
Available wherever books and ebooks are sold

THOMAS NELSON
Since 1798

thomasnelson.com